Tiger Country

This was first published 2011 by Areté *Books*
An imprint of Areté Ltd
8 New College Lane, Oxford OX1 3BN
Limited company 03876680; VAT Number 990 6680 78

www.aretemagazine.com

ISBN 978-0-9562739-4-9

Typset and printed by the Information Press, Southfield Road,
Eynsham, Oxford OX29 4JB

Cover design by Richard van den Dool.

CAUTION

Amateur Performing Rights

Applications for performance, including readings and excerpts, by amateurs
in English throughout the world should be addressed to the Performing
Rights Manager, Nick Hern Books, 14 Larden Road, London W3 7ST, tel
+44 (0)20 8749 4953, fax +44 (0)20 8735 0250, e-mail info@nickhernbooks.
demon.co.uk, except as follows:

Australia: Dominie Drama, 8 Cross Street, Brookvale 2100, fax (2) 9938 8695,
e-mail drama@dominie.com.au

New Zealand: Play Bureau, PO Box 420, New Plymouth, fax (6) 753 2150, e-
mail play.bureau.nz@xtra.co.nz

South Africa: DALRO (pty) Ltd, PO Box 31627, 2017 Braamfontein, tel (11)
712 8000, fax (11) 403 9094, e-mail theatricals@dalro.co.za

United States of America and Canada: United Agents, see details below

Professional Performing Rights

Application for performance by professionals in any medium and in any lan-
guage throughout the world (and amateur and stock rights in the USA and
Canada) should be addressed to United Agents, 12–26 Lexington Street, London W1F 0LE, fax +44 (0)20 3214 0801, e-mail info@unitedagents.co.uk

No performance of any kind may be given unless a licence has been obtained.
Applications should be made before rehearsals begin. Publication of this play
does not necessarily indicate its availability for amateur performance.

Nina Raine

Tiger Country

Areté*Books*

DRAMATIS PERSONAE

DOCTORS
Vashti (Urology Registrar) mid 30s, Indian, RP
John (Cardiology Registrar) mid/late 30s
Brian (Urology Consultant: Junior) mid/late 30s

Emily (Senior House Officer: just qualified, A&E), 27
Mark (SHO, Surgical) late 20s
James (SHO, Surgical) late 20s
Rebecca (House Officer) mid 20s
Mr Leffe (Senior Consultant, A&E), 50s

PATIENTS
These are all late/middle aged unless indicated
Mrs Bracken 60/70 upwards.
Gillian 60/70
Gillian's husband 60/70
Bindu 50s
Mr Mercer 60/70 upwards

OTHER HOSPITAL STAFF
Lakshmi (Theatre Sister) middle-aged
Olga (Senior Nurse) middle-aged
Comfort (Nurse)
Rosie (Senior Nurse) middle-aged

Anaesthetists, radiographers, porters, paramedics, other nurses etc
to be played by members of the company

Staff can and should play patients – doubling as follows:
Olga/Mrs Bracken/Gillian/various nurses (60s)
Anaesthetist/Gillian's husband/Mr Leffe/Mr Mercer (60s)
Lakshmi/Bindu/Surgical Reg/various nurses (40s)
Rebecca/Comfort/nurse (late 20s)
John/Paramedic (late 30s)
Brian/Man off a ladder/male nurse (mid-late 30s)
Vashti/24 year old girl

The play can be done with a cast of ten.

Tiger Country was first performed at the Hampstead Theatre, London, on 14 January 2011. The cast, in order of appearance, was as follows:

Thusitha Jayasundera	*Vashti*
Henry Lloyd-Hughes	*James*
Harvey Virdi	*Lakshmi/Bindu/Orthopaedic registrar*
Nicolas Tennant	*Brian/Man off a ladder*
David Cann	*Geoffrey Mercer/Mr Leffe/*
	Mrs Bracken's husband/Anaethetist
Sharon Duncan-Brewster	*Rebecca/Comfort*
Pip Carter	*Mark*
Joan Kempson	*Gillian/Olga*
Ruth Everett	*Emily*
Adam James	*John/Paramedic*
Maggie McCarthy	*Mrs Bracken/Rosie*
Nason Crone	*Orthopaedic surgeon/Porter*
Kevin Kamara	*Orthopaedic surgeon/Porter*
Naomi Heffernan	*Nurse/Orthopaedic surgeon*
Hannah Banister	*24 year old girl*

Nina Raine	*Director*
Lizzie Clachan	*Designer*
Rick Fisher	*Lighting Designer*
Fergus O'Hare	*Sound Designer*
Dick Straker	*Video Designer*
Jane Gibson	*Associate and Movement Director*
Hannah Banister	*Assistant Director*
Laura Flowers	*Stage Manager*
Sarah Tryfan	*Deputy Stage Manager*
Daisy Gladstone	*Assistant Stage Manager*
Heidi Lennard	*Company Stage Manager*

NOTE ON THE STAGING

The stage to be left as minimal as possible. A neutral, dark, empty space, that can shrink or expand as it is lit. One set of swinging doors, at the back. Since everything in a hospital is on wheels (chairs, beds, drips, trolleys of equipment), these are wheeled into scenes as required. Doors, when specified, need not be represented literally.

When we enter the invasive, investigative world of the hospital, as in the operations, and particularly when the echo-cardiogram is carried out, the images the doctors see should if possible be blown up as back projections.

With thanks to:

My family.

All at Kingston Hospital, Queen Victoria Hospital East Grinstead, John Radcliffe Hospital Oxford, St Mary's Hospital Paddington, and Queen's Hospital, Burton on Trent.

Thank you to all the doctors who talked to me so frankly, particularly Emilie Strawson, Roger Davies, Gus Gazzard, David James, and Peter Friend.

Special thanks also go to: Robin Fox and Amina Dasmal, Henri Lambert, Simon White, St John Donald, Matthew Byam Shaw, Janet Powell, Maria Dawson, Leon Baugh, Thomas Gray, Ramin Gray, Paraskevas Paraskeva, Ed Dick, Claire Lowdon and Sasha Slater.

Thank you to Nick Moseley and the students of Central School of Speech and Drama: Matthew Alexander, Shenae Anderson, Nason Crone, Abby Eletz, David Fairs, Naomi Heffernan, Ashley Hunter, Kevin Kamara, Catherine Lochran, Alexander Neal, David Portman, Henry Profitt, Chris Pybus, Christopher Rowland, and Rosie Woodham.

Many thanks to Stephen Brett and the Intensive Care Society.

And finally, but most particularly, my thanks go to John Dick, for your unquestioning help, generosity and amused patience, Phil Morgan and of course, Jyoti Shah. I could not have written this script without you.

For Nicky and Maya

Nina Raine

Tiger Country

ACT ONE

A DAY IN THE LIFE

Vashti sits, with a polystyrene cup of tea in her hands. Next to her stands James, a junior doctor. She drains her cup, squints at the bottom of it.

VASHTI

Ever read your tea-leaves?

JAMES

Can't say I do.

VASHTI

My grandfather used to read mine.

Out in Bhopal. He was the town healer.

A pause. James holds out a purple form.

JAMES

You'll be pleased to see the purple form.

VASHTI

I see the purple form – but it's not... (*she inspects her watch*) ...
eight o'clock yet, thank you.

(*She does not take the purple form, but swirls her cup, looking
into it*)

He'd go like this...

He'd cover the cup with his hand... he had massive hands...
(*she covers the top of the cup with her hand*) like this... read off
the vibe, the atmo... and he'd go... (*Taking her hand off, inspect-
ing the bottom of the cup, speaks in an Indian accent*) 'Ah, I see...
Behta... You are going to heal people... just like me, Vashti. You
have a pain in your shoulder – I feel where it is, with my hand
– until I feel the pain in my shoulder. I take away your pain.'

(*They laugh. She stands up, stretches.*)

Maybe I should try it.

JAMES

A shaman, was he?

VASHTI

A bullshitter. Still, it worked; I believed it all when I was ten.

(*She looks at her watch. 8 o'clock. Takes the purple form, squints
at it.*)

'Not for resuscitation.'

Who?

JAMES

Mr Doon.

VASHTI

Oh, God.

And I suppose I'd better go and talk to him.

(*She looks out.*)

What a lovely way to start the week.

She takes the form, signs it. As she does so, people appear around her, with a roaring surge in the sounds of the hospital.

LAKSHMI

Patient's ready. Good to go?

BRIAN

(*In scrubs, crossing the stage as he ties on a cap*) Can't find my effing clogs!

Mr Leffe is looking in a brown folder. He smiles.

MR LEFFE

(*Holding up an X-Ray to the light*) Mr Hall, I have good news for you. No sign of any cancer.

REBECCA

(*To no one in particular*) I've got a lady, 65, no known cardiac history, presenting complaint chest pains, can I refer her to one of the medics please?

OLGA

(*Loudly*) Ethel? Can you hear me? Do you want to open your eyes for me and see who's talking to you?

MARK

(*Out*) 'We don't have a bed' never means 'We don't have a bed.' If I get angry, you'll find me a bed.

He starts to dial a number into a phone.

JAMES

(*Looking at a patient's notes*) God, not another one. (*To Lakshmi, passing by*) Everyone's trying to kill themselves today.

John, coming on from the other side of the stage, also to Lakshmi

JOHN

Chest drain to do on the guy / in seven.

ANAESTHETIST

(*Urgently, pushing his head round a door*) /OK, she's arrested, can we put out a crash call please?

The assorted alarms of the crash call sound out. A flurry of activity.

ROSIE

(*Her voice amplified over a tannoy*) Can we have an SHO in resuss now, /please?

A bed is wheeled through the doors, people around it so we cannot see who is in it.

REBECCA

(*Running across the stage in the opposite direction*) /OK, OK, I heard you! I've got no trolley, no drugs, how the fuck am I meant to lead an arrest?

As she passes James she grabs his stethoscope off him.

JAMES

/Hey!

REBECCA

(*Without stopping*) I've got a crash call /coming.

OLGA

(*Crossing hurriedly in opposite direction, proffering a bag of blood*) Who wanted blood?

A knot of people has gathered around the bed.

ANAESTHETIST

(*At the head of the bed, he is wearing surgical hat and scrubs*) What's her history? Does anyone know what drugs she's on? We need to know who's leading this arrest!

REBECCA

(*Arriving at the bed*) I'm leading this arrest!

ANAESTHETIST

Then start bloody leading it!

MARK

(*Standing apart, on his own, into the phone*) No, you see, 'We don't have a bed' means, 'In ten minutes there'll be a bed', it means, 'We've got a bed, but there's a dead person in it'.

So get me a fucking /bed!

The defibrillator has arrived at the bedside.

OLGA

/There are too many people round this bed!

Everyone ignores her.

REBECCA

(*Holding pads aloft*) I'm clear, clear at the end, clear at the sides, everyone clear, oxygen away, shocking at 200, go!!

She plunges the pads down and with the electric shock, we freeze.

OPERATING THEATRE

Mark is at the operating theatre sinks, scrubbing up, showing Emily how to do it.

MARK

Scrub from the hand down to your elbows. And let the water drip down. That way the bugs drip off your elbows. Not down onto your hands. Then you turn the tap off with your elbow. (*He does so*) Not with your hands or you have to start all over again.

EMILY

Yes, I know. I'm not going to be doing anything, anyway.

MARK

Vashti never lets anyone do anything. All I'm allowed to do is stitch up after her. (*He mimes, camp fussy stitching*) 'Home Sweet Home.' So – where were you before?

EMILY

Brighton. Care of the Elderly.

MARK

And they've put you straight on call for general, covering A&E?

EMILY

Yes.

MARK

Let's hope you're a quick learner. It won't be like Care of the Crumble on Sea.

(*He strides over to a small, sterile parcel that has been unfolded for him and lies on the top of a small trolley – a theatre gown. He gingerly pulls on the gown.*)

Do me up.

Emily grudgingly ties the ties at the back of the gown. Mark has his forearms crossed across his chest, his fingertips pointing to his shoulders.

EMILY

Why've you got your arms like that?

MARK

To keep myself sterile.

EMILY

Do I get one?

MARK

No.

EMILY

(*Shuddering*) It's freezing in here.

MARK

And each of these costs £30. £10 quid to make, £20 to sterilise. It's not a bloody cardigan.

Emily and Mark make their way over from the sinks to the operating area, where the patient lies on the operating table. He is mostly covered in blue paper tenting, only the narrow strip of flesh just above his crotch is revealed. Vashti is already busy there. Not masked. At her side stand the theatre sister, Lakshmi, and the senior nurse, Rosie, passing her instruments. Masked.

VASHTI

(*Without looking up, curtly*) You're late. We've already started.

MARK

This is Emily. She's here to observe?

VASHTI

(*Curtly*) Whatever.

The atmosphere is intent, concentrated. A short pause during which Vashti works briskly, with quick, jerky movements. We cannot see what she is doing but hear the sharp 'tsst' as she cauterises the edges of the incision, and the hum of the equipment monitoring the patient. The anaesthetist, masked, stands at the head of the patient, studying this equipment for any signs of disruption. But all is calm. Mark inhales the smell of the cauterised flesh.

MARK

Mmm...someone burnt my bacon.

VASHTI

(*Ignoring him*) So ladies, we're taking out this man's wasted testicle...

(*Pause*)

Lakshmi, can I have the self-retainer, please...

(*Mark has positioned himself at the other side of the patient and starts to help, taking the clamp from Lakshmi and using it to hold the incision open for Vashti.*)

So I'm making the incision through the roof of the inguinal canal to get to the spermatic cord...

And we'll deliver it out that way. What are the layers of the abdomen?

EMILY

(*Taken by surprise*) Oh. Er. Me?

VASHTI

Ye-es.

EMILY

Starting from the top? Um, epidermis. Er. Superficial fascia.

Deep fascia.

VASHTI

And?

EMILY

Oh. Um, muscle.

VASHTI

(*Stopping suddenly*) Look, I know I'm a short arse, but does this table feel a little high?

Lakshmi suddenly comes to life.

LAKSHMI

Don't talk to me about that table. You know it's officially been condemned? I've been asking for a new one for 5 years. I thought we were going to get one at last, then I hear that apparently, the money's been diverted to a broken eye table. It really gets on my tits.

(*To Emily*) You're not sterile. Put some music on.

Emily obediently starts to shuffle through CDs.

Yes, they cost twenty grand but it lasts you twenty years. With this all we need is one obese patient and that'll finish it off. Don't put on carols. Just don't. I can't face it. Not until next week at least.

EMILY

...Then it's going to have to be *All Woman*?

She puts on a CD. A pop-song starts to play, softly.

LAKSHMI

You look at the money they give to the bastards in chemotherapy. The drugs are ongoing. And we're operating on a 27-year-old condemned table.

Brian comes in.

BRIAN

Oh God. (*He picks up the CD case*) Not *All Woman* again. Do we have to? I've got my Ipod, (*he pulls it out, starts scrolling through it*) – we could have *The Lion King* –

LAKSHMI

Sorry mate. You're outnumbered.

There are two of you (*indicating Brian and Mark*) and four of us.

BRIAN

Yes – there's way too much oestrogen around here today.

LAKSHMI

So it'll be *All Woman.*

BRIAN

(*Noting Emily*) Hello.

EMILY

(*Introducing herself*) Emily.

BRIAN

Hold on, what about the patient? He's a man.

LAKSHMI

He doesn't count.

Brian wanders over to the operating table, peers over Vashti's shoulder.

BRIAN

We in business?

VASHTI

(*Abstractedly*) Fine. (*She tugs at something*) I'm just getting at his cord.

Brian goes into a little side room, we hear the tinny chord as he starts up his computer to check his emails.

VASHTI

God, I need a coffee. Mark, you can make us all one after this.

MARK

Why is it *always* me who makes the coffee?

VASHTI

Because I'm the reg and you're my SHO.

MARK

It's CT2, Vashti, that's what we're called now.

VASHTI

Whatever, Mark. (*Points to herself*) Senior ‒ (*Points to him*) Junior. It's called a hierarchy.

(*Resuming her teacherly tone*) And when we've taken out the wasted testicle, we replace it with what?

They look at her blankly.

EMILY

Do you have to replace it with anything?

MARK

Can't he just have one ball?

VASHTI

Would you like one ball? ‒ Oh sorry, I forgot. You don't have any, do you.

LAKSHMI

Here. False balls.

(*Rosie lifts up the false balls from the trolley. They look like small, clear plastic eggs and they are each in their own vacuum pack.*)

ROSIE

Vashti, we've got small, medium and large. Which will you be using?

MARK

Large.

VASHTI

(*Coldly*) Small.

MARK

(*Takes it*) Cool!

VASHTI

Put it down, will you? (*Struggling*) I can't...quite...get at the...

Lakshmi. I think I'm going to have to open this up a bit more.

Mark, you can stop arsing around and make yourself useful. Get ready to swab.

Mark stands next to her with a swab in his hand. Lakshmi passes Vashti the diathermy probe. Vashti lengthens the incision. She quickly starts to cauterise the wound.

VASHTI

Swab.

Swab.

Lakshmi, I need more retraction. I can't see... what I'm doing...

(*Mark swabs in the wound.*)

OK. Get another. Quick.

I said get another!

LAKSHMI

Is everything all right?

Beat

VASHTI

I've lost it... I've lost the bleeding-point.

Suddenly everyone is tense. Mark scurries round, gets another swab, Lakshmi also comes forward and hovers with a swab. Emily hovers impotently − she is not sterile. A brief, tense silence as they work.

EMILY

Can I do anything?

MARK

Shit, he's really bleeding

VASHTI

(*To Mark*) Get out of the way! How can I cauterise if you're in my way?

MARK

But you told me to swab!

VASHTI

(*A note of real panic in her voice*) Brian, he's *bleeding.*

Brian immediately emerges from the side room where he was tinkering at his computer.

I just can't find what's bleeding −

BRIAN

OK. Let me just –

(*He doesn't bother scrubbing up properly, just pulls on sterile gloves, extremely swiftly and as he does so instructs* –)

Just try and get rid of the blood so we can see –

Vashti's bleep goes off. Everyone ignores it. Lakshmi is swabbing. So is Vashti. Mark passes swabs. A scratchy voice comes over the intercom.

INTERCOM

Patient's here.

LAKSHMI

(*In direction of intercom*) Alright, thank you.

Brian comes hastily up, takes over from Vashti who hovers at his elbow, nervously. The bleep bleeps again, louder, since no one has intercepted the page. They are all intent over the patient. Mark continues to swab, so does Vashti.

BRIAN

Don't worry –

I'll see if we can... find what's bleeding... –

INTERCOM: Could someone answer the Urologist's bleep please.

LAKSHMI

(*In direction of intercom*) She's scrubbed and busy in theatre.

INTERCOM

Thank you.

BRIAN

Ah.

Can I have a mosquito please...

....and load me a dunlop, please...

LAKSHMI

(*To Rosie*) Two Oh Vicral

Rosie empties the sterile needle pack out of its packaging onto the trolly. Lakshmi passes Brian a threaded needle. Brian starts to put in a stitch.

VASHTI

He...

BRIAN

There we go...

(*Another pause, everyone still intent.*)

That should... should do the trick...

There.

(*Vashti walks away and stands by herself, looking at Brian and the patient from a little distance. Looks away.*)

Vashti.

VASHTI

Yes.

BRIAN

It's OK now. You can take it from here.

VASHTI

Thanks.

But she doesn't move.

CARDIOLOGY

John and Olga in a private room. There is a man sitting on the bed – Mr Mercer – thin, naked from the waist up. His jaw is sagging strangely, in fact his whole body looks strange and sagging. He is very sick.

JOHN

(*Carefully drawing up the plunger of the syringe, he injects it into a bag and connects a venflon*)

You know how much this stuff costs?

MR MERCER

How much?

JOHN

800 quid a pop. You've got all the pharmacists on our backs, know that?

MR MERCER

Ahh...but I'm 'worth it' aren't I?

They laugh, which turns into a rattling cough in his case.

JOHN

You know you've got a crazy fan in here? Olga wants to get your autograph.

OLGA

John! I didn't mean now.

MR MERCER

Not a problem.

Beat while John works.

OLGA

I do watch it every week.

...Is Doctor Patel going to come back? I liked him.

MR MERCER

There's a vague rumour.

JOHN

So, you know the drill. We're going to find our way in with a wire and drain you off a bit.

MR MERCER

Last week it was yellow.

JOHN

Yellow is good.

MR MERCER

So what's bad?

JOHN

Anything else. Blood. Lego. White picket fence...

They laugh.

Right, ready to go I think.

MR MERCER

You're the boss.

He looks off at an angle, to distract himself. John carries on, busily. Because he is working, from his back we can't really see what he's doing.

OLGA

So can you tell us the story-lines coming up?

MR MERCER

More than my job's worth... Nah, you create it yourself to a certain extent. The writers lead you and then they follow your lead.

OLGA

Do you ad-lib or is it all in the script?

MR MERCER

Oh no, there's a script and you stick to it.

OLGA

I think they should give you a bit of romance. A nurse or something.

MR MERCER

So do I, darling.

(*Mr Mercer's breathing is laboured. It is obvious his lungs are swimming with fluid.*)

I'm going to cough now, is that all right?

JOHN

Help yourself.

(*He coughs. John winces.*)

Ooh, got a lot of fluid there, haven't you?

OLGA

I cried. When Josie died.

MR MERCER

I know. I still get letters.

OLGA

Did it affect you? I mean, in an emotional way?

MR MERCER

Sort of. Sometimes, do a very upsetting scene, it gets in your bones.

Olga forces the plastic packaging from the sterile syringes and paraphernalia into her overflowing bin.

OLGA

This bin needs emptying.

MR MERCER

Like me.

JOHN

(*To Olga*) Bit more local please.

She passes him another syringe. A short silence.

MR MERCER

Think I've got pain now. Up here.

JOHN

Yeah that's because...when I touch your diaphragm, you feel the pain up there in your shoulder...Weird, but that's how we're wired...

(*He carries on manipulating the wire, then feeds a tube up it.*)

There we go.

Another short silence.

MR MERCER

I feel sick.

JOHN

(*To Olga*) Get him a bowl.

(*Olga goes to the sink and brings back a grey cardboard dish. She puts it on Mr Mercer's lap.*)

That's because the wire is... stimulating certain nerves. The pain response is to feel sick. (*To Olga*) Give him something for the sickness. 50mg cyclizine.

Another short silence, during which Olga takes a venflon, flushes the venflon with saline and then injects cyclizine.

MR MERCER

(*Weakly*) Got something for everything, haven't you?

JOHN

We do.

OLGA

We'll have you back on telly in no time.

JOHN

You should feel better in a moment.

– Don't blame you actually, I'd feel sick if I was having that done.

MR MERCER

(*To Olga*) My turn next week, you hold him down.

(*They laugh.*)

(*John reaches behind Mr Mercer and we see the beaker, behind Mr Mercer's back, filled with fluids from his chest. There is blood in it. John and Olga meet each other's eyes as Olga takes it from him.*)

Is there blood?

OPERATING THEATRE

Brian is still at the side of the patient. He is just completing the first stitch to close the last layer of the wound in the patient's skin. The Lion King is now playing – 'Circle of Life'. Vashti is nowhere to be seen. Emily watches silently.

BRIAN

Kids! (*Brian and Mark laugh*) All surgeons want to be *plastic* surgeons when they grow up... all medics want to be *neurologists* when they grow up...and all kids want to be *lions.*

Can I have a suture...

And forceps please...

(*Lakshmi passes him a threaded needle*)

Arhhh... can someone scratch my nose please...

(*Emily hesitantly does so.*)

That's right... that's it... just there.

Right. I've put in the first stitch. Mark. Do you want to have a go at doing him up?

Mark, who has been eagerly hovering, moves forward with alacrity.

MARK

Great.

BRIAN

Just make sure your stitches are the same size, you'll be OK.

Meanwhile Lakshmi is counting the bloody swabs out in fives, muttering under her breath as she counts. Emily holds out a yellow plastic bag for the swabs to go into.

The music on the Ipod changes to a catchy tune: We No Speak Americano. *Imperceptibly, everyone starts to bob in time to the music.*

Brian holds up the plastic kidney bowl with the forlorn, bloody testicle in it.

BRIAN

Anyone want his testicle?

MARK

Vashti. She collects them.

LAKSHMI

(*Firmly, taking the kidney bowl*) One for the theatre dog, I think.

They exchange a look. Vashti comes in from the sinks, pulling on a pair of gloves.

VASHTI

Hi.

(*Beat. Mark sings softly under his breath – 'Hitler has only got one ball'.*)

Where are we at?

(*She comes over to Mark busy working on the patient. Watches him.*)

You shouldn't be holding the needle in your fingers, Mark. You should get used to tying with an instrument.

MARK

Yeah, but... it makes it more difficult.

VASHTI

That's why you should get used to it.

(*Lakshmi passes him the relevant instrument, silently. This hampers Mark's progress considerably. A pause while Vashti watches Mark labour, in silence.*)

It's easier if you stand on the side you're stitching.

BRIAN

He's halfway through now.

Vashti watches, with contained impatience, as Mark sews. Suddenly –

VASHTI

Oh God let me do it.

She takes the needle and starts to work, very quickly.

BRIAN

I said Mark could do it.

VASHTI

Brian, look at this. (*She indicates*) Mark. You're meant to try and make the skin meet the skin again. (*She gestures*) If I left it like that he'd end up with one hell of a scar.

She busies herself.

MARK

How am I going to learn if you won't let me practise?!

BRIAN

Mark, calm down.

VASHTI

Listen, Mark. The only thing the patient sees is the scar. He won't see what a great job we've done inside. Just the scar. So the scar had better be good. And this scar is going to be crap.

She continues to work. Mark storms out of theatre, tearing off his theatre gown as he goes. Emily watches him go.

A&E

James is with Emily. She is talking conspiratorially, exhilarated.

EMILY

Shitting myself! I've already discharged five people and it's not even ten o'clock.

JAMES

Perfect. Get 'em out of here. Then see if you can sneak out and watch me operate.

EMILY

I've already seen one. The guy who walked me in was a twat. Are you all like that?

JAMES

No!

EMILY

But A&E's bloody terrifying. I love it. I'm making it up as I go along. Everyone's go*t chest* pain –

JAMES

Got your bible?

She looks at her hand, which is gripping a green and yellow book – the Oxford Medical Handbook.

EMILY

Oh yeah. Yeah! I haven't let go of the cheese and onion all morning. (*She brandishes it*) It's fantastic. It's the only thing that's keeping me together.

– But then this *dick* of a radiographer – refusing to give me a second x-ray – you should have seen the one I got, it was blurry, it was crap – I felt like saying, look, mate, this is *why* you're a radiographer, not a doctor, because you're a lazy shit –

JAMES

Babe listen to me. (*He puts his hands on her waist*) There's absolutely no point –

EMILY

– I know but –

JAMES

− In getting angry with them −

EMILY

− I didn't −

JAMES

Especially not if you're a young ladeee. I know this place.

(*Beat*)

It just means they take you less seriously, not more.

EMILY

I didn't say it. I just felt like saying it.

JAMES

Don't bother even feeling it.

Mr Leffe and Brian walk in, mid-conversation. Mr Leffe is older − a consultant. He is imposing, authoritative.

MR LEFFE

...It's been dragging on for weeks, upshot is, she doesn't want surgery on her gall bladder − because she's been told she'll get diarrhoea.

(*They laugh.*)

We're never going to get rid of her!

BRIAN

Tell you what, let's swap. Swap her with one of mine.

MR LEFFE

Done.

BRIAN

Shake on it.

They shake hands, and laugh again.

MR LEFFE

Oh God, am I going to regret this? What am I getting?

BRIAN

(*With an ironic expansiveness*) No, mine's wonderful. 87-year-old, been here two months, she's stopped eating and drinking and wants to die.

They both burst out laughing.

MR LEFFE

(*Ruefully*) Fair enough. Fair enough. (*As Mr Leffe strides past Emily and James, they both visibly straighten*)

JAMES

Good morning, Mr Leffe.

MR LEFFE

Ah. Gather we'll be seeing you skiing this weekend, James.

JAMES

Absolutely.

MR LEFFE

Good, good. Very much looking forward.

Mr Leffe is about to walk on.

EMILY

Mr Leffe, can I introduce myself? I'm your new on-call SHO. (*She sticks out her hand. Mr Leffe does not take it.*)

MR LEFFE

Sorry, your name is...?

EMILY

Emily Logan.

MR LEFFE

The new SHO?

EMILY

Yes.

MR LEFFE

Where were you this morning? At 8.30? When we went round last night's take?

EMILY

I know, Mr Leffe. I'm sorry about that. It was a failure of communication between my last hospital and this one. I only finished there at midnight last night, they couldn't change my shift.

Beat

MR LEFFE

I see. A pleasure to have you with us. (*He shakes her hand*) Good morning.

He goes.

JAMES

See, you got away with it.

EMILY

Got away with what? It was the truth. – *Skiing?* He's not even your consultant, he's mine, you *operator*!

JAMES

No, *my* consultant wangled a research freebie in Geneva. I couldn't say no.

EMILY

I thought we were going to have this weekend together.

Beat.

JAMES

Babe, it'll be different now.

EMILY

How?

JAMES

We'll see each other all the time.

(*Beat*)

We won't be able to get away from each other.

BLADDER CLINIC

Vashti sits at a desk. A small bare room. Comfort, a West Indian nurse, stands by the door. By the end of Vashti's speech James has put on a white coat, and joined her.

VASHTI

...*And* I'm supposed to be completing on a house. How am I meant to do that when I look at people's bladders and willies all day? (*She gets up, starts striding around the room*) I don't know how to buy a *house*. If it's not a willy, I don't know what to do with it. Comfort – you're called Comfort aren't you?

COMFORT

(*Heavily*) Yes.

VASHTI

How about shutting the door properly in here?

Right, who's our first patient? I don't seem to have their notes here, Comfort.

Comfort is still struggling with the door.

COMFORT

No?

VASHTI

I need the notes before I can see the patients. Comfort.

COMFORT

I didn't know...

VASHTI

(*Goes to a weighty computer in the corner of the room*) Would you be able to look up on the system –

COMFORT

No.

VASHTI

'No.' She wouldn't be able to look it up on the system. OK. (*Under her breath, but audible*) Not very 'Comfort' –ing, is she?

(*To Comfort*) It delays the clinic if the notes aren't there.

(*She starts to tap into the computer.*)

This isn't really what I'm here for.

(*She scrolls down the screen.*)

Oh for God's bloody sake! We've got another one.

JAMES

Another one what?

VASHTI

'Wet woman.' It's the same boring story every time. (*She scrolls through the notes*) 65, three children, suffering from urinary incontinence, bladi bladi bladi bladder. God, I hate them. What do they expect? It's their own stupid fault. (*As if to an imbecile*) 'Stop having babies. Then you won't get wet.'

JAMES

Bit of a drastic solution.

VASHTI

No. I'm going to get my tubes tied next year.

JAMES

(*Genuinely taken aback*) No way!

VASHTI

Yes way.

JAMES

Why?

VASHTI

Why do you think? Because I don't want kids. That's why.

(*Turning away from the computer, she picks up a single piece of paper on the desk.*)

What's this? Something I'm meant to fill in?

COMFORT

(*Leaving the door, coming over*) Yes.

VASHTI

(*With barely suppressed irritation*) Well how am I meant to know? Do I have to guess everything? I'm not psychic.

COMFORT

I thought it was a regular thing.

VASHTI

(*Curtly*) No.

(*She goes to a trolley*) K.Y.?

COMFORT

I didn't...

VASHTI

I'm going to *need* it, aren't I, if I'm going to feel anyone's prostate.

(*She waves some very large plastic gloves.*)

As well as some gloves in my size. (*She holds her hand up, wiggles her fingers*) Small. Not gardening gloves.

(*Beat*)

Can you get me the gloves and the lubrication and the notes please!

(*Comfort exits, wordlessly. Vashti turns to the desk, to start filling in the form. She mutters to herself.*)

How am I meant to run a clinic without the notes, without K.Y., without a nurse who knows her arse from her elbow. NHS again, *innit*. Great, *innit*.

CARDIOLOGY: CHEST CLINIC

John. Sitting in clinic. He is on his mobile phone. Taking a chicken sandwich out of its packaging at the same time. Throughout the whole of the scene he is prevented from ever taking a bite of it.

JOHN

...I'm in clinic.

(*His bleep goes off – a different pitch to the normal one.*)

Just my bleep.

(*We hear a crackly voice saying 'adult cardiac arrest Bronte ward, adult cardiac arrest Bronte ward'.*)

No. They've forgotten to cancel my on-call.

(*He silences it.*)

Cardiac arrest.

I don't care. Let the shit hit the fan. Highlight the cracks in the system.

No. Actually I was ringing about –

(*Nodding* Yeah)

Sort of... (*he feels his neck*)... gooseberry size.

(*Beat*)

I know, I know, so you're saying, sooner the better.

(*Beat*)

OK, OK. Point taken. Thanks.

(*Beat*)

No, I mean I feel fine at the moment.

(*The bleep goes off again. He looks at it, silences it.*)

' – Be on the safe side.' Yeah.

(*Ironically*) Yeah, yeah, yeah, I'm shitting myself.

(*He makes to have a bite of his chicken sandwich. The phone on his desk rings.*)

Sorry, Brian, can you hold on a minute?

(*He picks up the other phone.*)

Hello.

Chest pains?

(*Beat*)

Ahh, you know what to do.

(*Beat*)

Ah give her air. Give her...

Give her a pack of cigarettes.

(*He laughs.*)

OK. Call me if you need to.

(*He puts the phone down, picks up the mobile again.*)

Sorry about that.

A nurse comes in. Puts a pile of patients' notes on his desk. John is about to take a bite of his chicken sandwich.

NURSE

Patient's waiting. Shall I send him in?

Beat

JOHN

This has to be the longest time it's ever – taken anyone – to eat a chicken sandwich.

(*The nurse waits, neutrally. John puts down sandwich, starts wearily leafing through notes.*)

Why not. Why not.

The nurse goes out.

THE DOCTORS' MESS

Noise. Pop music. The Doctors' mess is like a students' common room. A kitchen area with chairs and tables and a lounging area with sofas, and a huge television showing MTV. There are vending machines for coke, chocolate, sandwiches. A microwave. A strange mix of recent expense and dilapidation.

Some doctors sing rowdily along with the song on the telly – Beyoncé. Rebecca, a good-looking girl, much in evidence, dancing on a coffee table. Dissolving into laughter, they break it up. Rebecca goes over to Mark who is playing darts on his own

REBECCA

You know why it is, Mark. Because you keep going behind her back.

MARK

Vashti is an asexual surgical bitch who shits on her juniors and brown-noses the consultants. There's nothing behind the eyes. She's a 'Dead Doc'.

REBECCA

Yeah, yeah, yeah. You don't like being bossed around by a girl. Well when Vashti finds out what you've done on the ward you're fucking *dead*.

MARK

What have I done on the ward?

REBECCA

Oh come on Mark. I just heard from one of the nurses that you used an introducer on that patient when Vashti specifically told you not to.

Beat

MARK

So sue me.

REBECCA

Yeah. They could you know.

MARK

He needed to be catheterised.

REBECCA

You're gonna fucking get it, man. (*She makes a slitting throat gesture*)

MARK

Yeah but I did it fine!

REBECCA

But that's not the point! The point is, you're sticking a posh knitting-needle up the man's cock! It could end up anywhere! It's a very delicate tube. It's a penis. I mean, I've heard the penis is a delicate tube. Maybe I'm wrong. Perhaps you could tell me. Jesus, Mark, I couldn't believe it when I'd heard you'd done it on your own.

MARK

I did it on my own, and it was fine. Why is everyone so paralysed by this place? Fuck it, we have to make decisions on our own, without consultants, every minute of the day. You have to do what you think best.

REBECCA

Mm, Apocalypse Now. Bullshit, Mark. There are hospital guidelines and if you go against them and are sued, you're liable. No one will support you if you do that.

MARK

And if you lived completely within the limits then you'd never do anything, would you?

REBECCA

(*Shrugging*) Don't say I didn't warn you.

Mark angrily throws another dart. The conversation is over. Rebecca moves to the eating area. MTV continues to play in the background. A group of doctors – as many of the actors as possible – are sitting in the eating area, a rowdy conversation in midflow. They are eating toast, drinking coffee. People milling about. There is a slightly hysterical air of licence. This is where the doctors let their hair down. John has wandered in and sets about making himself a coffee, silently, in the background. On another table Brian sits with Mark, also talking. Two separate conversations mid-flow.

JAMES

...So, he rings him up, and he says, (*Small dramatic beat*) 'Doctor, your patient's dead.' And he goes, 'Listen, (*small dramatic beat*) I may be good: but I'm not that good.'

They all burst out laughing.

REBECCA

Hey, gorgeous.

She pinches his bottom.

JAMES

/Ow!...

BRIAN

(*To Mark, mid-story*).../We started off trying to crush it, right, this enormous kidney stone –

MARK

And how big was it? (*Seeing John*) All right John mate.

BRIAN

(*Riffles through*) It's here, in his notes. Scary. You want to see it? (*He hands him a plastic sachet with a surprisingly large stone – the size of a cherry stone*)

MARK

(*Snorting with incredulous laughter*) I reckon you picked that up at the seaside.

BRIAN

Yup. The stone was actually *growing* faster than we were crushing it...

They laugh together. A bleep goes off, loudly. Everyone instinctively checks theirs, then relaxes. Back to the other table

JAMES

...She weighed 156 kilos, this *tsunami* of flesh, she had a haemoglobin of 4-5 which was pretty spectacular I thought, and I had to do her cos no one else wanted to, when we put her on the table we literally had to *strap* her to it – (*Makes circular motion with hands*)

REBECCA

– It was not pretty, there was a hell of a lot of tissue rolling towards us –

JAMES

– It was like Laurel and Hardy. I blew up the bags...

The bleep goes off again.

MARK

Who's lost their bleep? (*He gets up. It bleeps again, louder.*)

REBECCA

Where's it coming from?

JAMES

(*Facetiously*) Try looking in the microwave.

Mark opens the microwave with a flourish. Empty. The bleep gives its final, loudest bleep.

MARK

Aha. (*It is between two packets of cereal, on the side. He inspects the number bleeping.*)

REBECCA

Whose bleep? And who's bleeping?

MARK

Why don't you answer it, find out. 'Little Bo Peep has lost her bleep –'

REBECCA

He who finds the bleep, answers it.

MARK

Fuck's sake. (*He moves to the phone*) If I end up taking a G.P. referral...

JAMES

It'll be like, 'This is doctor – *chk!*' (*He mimes slamming down the phone*)

Brian turns to James.

BRIAN

(*Gesturing after Mark*) You know what he needs? A girlfriend.

MARK

(*Over his shoulder*) Yeah, yeah...

JAMES

Yes, and this place is like an enormous *hotel*...

REBECCA

What do you mean?

JAMES

All those nurses, all those on-call rooms...

MARK

(*From the phone, where he is busy standing and dialling*) Nurses aren't sexy anymore, they're all... Filipinos now. No, I'll tell you who the new nurses are, –

JAMES/MARK

(*In unison*) *Physios* are the new nurses.

REBECCA

A few years ago we would've been the nurses and you would be after us.

JAMES

(*Flirtatiously*) Jealous, are you?

REBECCA

Reminding you of the facts.

(*James raises his hands in supplication, leaves the mess.*)

There's this old guy on our ward, I've told him a zillion times, he still calls me nurse. He also gets a hard-on when I try to catheterise him, but that's by the by. My point is, he'll call some male nurse, I mean some queen like Matthew, 'Doctor'. – I like to address Matthew as 'Sister'. Push his buttons a bit.

BRIAN

You know that old male nurse, the one off Holby is here?

REBECCA

What, 'Bernard'?

Not 'Bernie'?

BRIAN

Yeah.

REBECCA

No way!

BRIAN

Know how much *he* gets paid? Hundred grand a year. I asked him.

REBECCA

Fucking hell! What ward? What's he in with? 'Bernie'! I love him!

Rebecca coughs.

BRIAN

That sounds nasty.

REBECCA

(*Washing some pills down*) I've already nicked some Erythromycin off the ward. (*She coughs again.*)

BRIAN

Self-medicating, tsk, tsk.

REBECCA

I've got to go and see Bernie. Tell him I'm in love with him. (*Looking through some notes*) What shall I prescribe this kid? I'm antibiotic-dyslexic today.

BRIAN

Smarties.

REBECCA

Crack.

MARK

(*Plumping himself back down, throwing the bleep on the table*) Belongs to the new surgical totty. Lost her bleep.

BRIAN

New totty! What's her 'history'?

MARK

You know. 'Emily'. In Vashti's op this morning.

BRIAN

Oh yes, very nice.

MARK

(*Shaking his head*) Stay clear. She's a ball-breaker.

BRIAN

Break yours, did she?

MARK

Kicked the radiographer's arse in A&E for doing an inadequate X-Ray.

REBECCA

Oh, Florence Nightingale, I met her.

MARK

Actually, she was right. He'd only done the top half of the pelvis.
Turned out she had a massive pelvic fracture, just out of the frame.
Bleeding internally.

BRIAN

(*Raising his eyebrows*) Good call. So Emily's got a good nose.
Aahh... (*He sips his coffee*) This is the life.

*There is a brief moment, as all the doctors silently enjoy their
coffee. Then Brian's bleep goes off. He groans, inspects it, gets up,
goes over to the phone and dials.*

REBECCA

(*Rousing herself, leafs through her magazine and finds the horo-
scopes*) Mark. I know that you act from the more primitive centres of
the brain – you're not a *frontal* lobe kind of guy – but am I correct in
thinking you're a Virgo?

(*Gleefully reading the magazine*) Well, 'You must learn to curb
your judgmental nature, and, once in a while, listen to those around
you. You –'

MARK

(*Grabbing magazine*) Fuck you. (*He reads, briefly*) Fuck's sake. (*Gets
up. Appeals to John*) Mate. You're a reg aren't you? Tell her it's bollocks.

JOHN

More things in heaven and earth. There's this friend of mine who
sees a clairvoyant, swears by her. She even got me to go.

Beat

MARK

(*Derisively*) You're a doctor, sweetie, I can't believe I'm hearing this. It's not the fucking Middle Ages. – Wait, wait... No, I can feel it... A hawthorn tree is calling me... And the water spirits are angry.

JOHN

No, I just thought, you know, I'd go as the sceptic and expose her.

REBECCA

What did she say?

Mark's bleep goes off. He looks at it.

MARK

She said, 'Time to head up to the ward.'

JOHN

Actually, just boring stuff, to begin with. There's a man in your life, he's still a virgin, he's called Mark, he needs help...

MARK

Fuck off...

JOHN

He will tell you to fuck off... No, it was all money, work, blah blah. Boring stuff.

Then suddenly she goes, who's this man with teeth in his hand going I'm a monster, I'm a monster?

And the thing is, my granddad, who'd died years ago, always used to get his false teeth out when I was little and go (*Makes snapping motion with hand*) 'I'm a monster, I'm a monster'.

Beat

REBECCA

Wow.

MARK

(*Forcefully*) It's all bullshit.

REBECCA

How can that be bullshit?

MARK

It's just about asking the right questions.

REBECCA

(*Gets up, grabs magazine back off Mark. To John*) What star sign are you?

JOHN

Virgo.

Vashti comes in.

REBECCA

I knew it! *Both* uptight Virgos! OK... (*She prepares to read the horoscope aloud*)

VASHTI

Mark. I need a word.

MARK

What?

VASHTI

In private, please.

(*Mark reluctantly gets up, moves a little distance away to talk to Vashti. This is not lost on the other doctors. There is a slight pause, while everyone surreptitiously listens to see what this is about.*)

Mark. You used an introducer on Mr Regan.

MARK

I know I did.

VASHTI

For God's sake Mark! I *specifically...*

She lowers her voice. From here we overhear snatches of their conversation, whenever one of them raises their voice. Their conversation is tense, vehement, and kept quiet only by some effort.

REBECCA

(*Throwing an expressive look in Mark's direction. Reading aloud*)
'Virgos. This won't be the easiest week of your life.'

In the corner, Mark makes a gesture of impatience.

MARK

You tell Lucy off for *not* catheterising Mr Doon. You tell me off for doing the opposite –

VASHTI

I'm 'telling you off' for disobeying me, Mark! I'm fed up with this. I'm fed up with your attitude, I'm fed up with you *cheeking* me all the time –

MARK

Just because you screwed up an operation this morning, Vashti, is no reason to take it out on me.

Beat. Everyone hears this.

VASHTI

This is your last warning, Mark. You're leaving me with no option but to report you to the consultants. To Mr Foster.

She walks out.

REBECCA

'...However, you may find surprising avenues open for you, romantically.'

(*Beat. Everyone is looking at Mark. He angrily walks out too. Someone whistles.*)

Fucking hell.

Is he in trouble?

BRIAN

No comment.

A beat. No one knows what to say. Emily walks into the mess.

EMILY

Oh, hooray. Is this my bleep? (*She picks up the bleep*) Yes, this is my bleep.

REBECCA

I've got to head. Read Bernie his horoscope. – Anyone know what floor he's on?

JOHN

Eleven. Room three.

REBECCA

Oh. His own room?

There's a moment of understanding.

JOHN

Yeah... Not going be with us for long.

A general exodus begins.

EMILY

(*Catching John, just picking up his bag to leave as well*) Oh – excuse me – are *you* the cardiology reg?

JOHN

Yes.

Emily and John are now the only people left in the mess.

EMILY

Oh, fantastic. Hi, I'm Emily. I've got a 60-year-old lady, presenting complaint palpitations and a burning sensation on drinking hot fluids, and I don't know whether to discharge her or not. She's just a bit vague about her symptoms.

JOHN

How long's it been going on for?

EMILY

She's not sure. I mean, I could be making a meal of it, I'm just going on a hunch...

But the thing is, I spoke to Dr West –

JOHN

Dr West?!

EMILY: I know, maybe I should have bleeped you first but the thing is he was in A&E anyway and someone mentioned he was the cardiology *consultant*... so, I went up to him and I said, this woman's getting a burning sensation and so on, and –

Well, when I'd finished he looked at me like I'd just, I don't know, shat on the floor.

(*John laughs and Emily does too.*)

He obviously thought I was being... he just said (*shortly*) 'Acid reflux or oesophagal candidiasis. Give her some anti-fungals and discharge her.'

(*John laughs again.*)

JOHN

He can be quite short.

EMILY

But the thing is as far as I'm concerned it's cardiac until proven otherwise.

(*Beat*)

She's got sudden shortness of breath... It could be something... I just don't want to discharge her and then for her to die on me, you know?

JOHN

You're new, aren't you?

EMILY

Yes, why?

JOHN

Just that... you're still worrying about people dying.

(*He looks at his watch, then sees her look.*)

No, I know. Every time you send a patient home you know what could happen.

(*Beat*)

But the thing is, it *will* happen. Eventually.

EMILY

It hasn't happened to me yet.

JOHN

But it will.

EMILY

But it hasn't yet.

JOHN

But the sooner you get used to that idea, the better.

(*Beat*)

You can't save everyone.

THE CONSULTANTS' OFFICE

A tiny office. Brian and Vashti, alone.

BRIAN

How much is it that you just don't like him?

VASHTI

Brian, you've *seen* him. He answers me back, argues with me, at the drop of a hat. It's unacceptable. Once you break down the hierarchy it allows for debate. And I'm not having *that*. Not with him.

BRIAN

Vashti.

VASHTI

If I don't get him first, he'll get me. I'm going to have a word with the other consultants about him.

BRIAN

Vashti, you mismanage him. You –

VASHTI

Hang on just a minute.

Hang *on*.

I 'mismanage' him?

How about him mismanaging me?

BRIAN

You're his senior. It's very easy to make his life hell. It's your responsibility not to.

VASHTI

I'm a doctor. That's my job. Mark's there to help me do my job. If I say 'please will you do this for me,' 'PLEASE will you check the bloods,' rather than 'Why haven't you checked the bloods, Mark, I asked you to three hours ago,' does it make me a better doctor?

BRIAN

Yes.

VASHTI

No.

Brian looks at her properly for a moment.

BRIAN

Jesus, you're really into shut-down, you know that? Is this all because you want that promotion? What's *happening* to you? No boyfriend, no sex, no children, no – when was the last time you had a good cry?

VASHTI

None of your business. Wanting to fuck me doesn't give you any rights, you know.

BRIAN

So I wanted to. Still do.

VASHTI

And I didn't. End of story.

I've been asked straight out. 'So what's he like in bed, then?'

BRIAN

So what? People talk. Deal with it. I do.

VASHTI

There's a difference, Brian.

BRIAN

What's the difference?

VASHTI

There's no way that *you* could be sleeping your way into your job. And that's probably why you've got the job.

BRIAN

You didn't apply.

VASHTI

Because I knew you would get it.

Fine. I can deal with it. And this time round, I'm applying.

It just means I don't have a sex life anymore. It's safer.

Just one more thing crossed off the list.

BRIAN

And you couldn't wait to cross it off.

VASHTI

In case you hadn't noticed, if you're a woman, children's what you do when your career hasn't worked out. Cos it'll finish it off for you. Joke.

BRIAN

You're full of jokes today.

VASHTI

I am. Put in a penny, I'll tell you a joke.

BRIAN

I don't want you to screw things up for yourself because people think you come across as arrogant.

VASHTI

You know, I'm fed up with being told I 'come across' as arrogant. I 'come across' as arrogant because I *am* arrogant.

Why can't I just be me?

BRIAN

Because you can't jackboot around your juniors, and then go running for backup to your seniors. Either you're the boss or you're not. You can't be both.

VASHTI

But I am both, Brian! I've got the worst of both worlds! I've got *crap* coming at me from the consultants, and *crap* coming at me from the juniors, and *crap* coming at me from the nurses, who resent the fact that I'm not a nurse, so they strop, if you don't say 'please' and 'thank you', they wait for the moment they can undermine you in front of a patient, and boy will they undermine you if they get a chance. And it's these fat, old, *vacuous* black nurses – Pardon me for saying so, but it's true –

(*Just as she says this a nurse passes and she is forced to lower her voice, which gradually rises again throughout the following.*)

– But, you're a woman, and so are they, and you're not white, and neither are they, so why do you think you can boss *them* around? This job is about being liked, by blokes, but men don't like women who act like blokes, and to be taken seriously as a surgeon you have to act like a bloke, so you're fucked. Or else it's some *wanker* in orthopaedics saying so how come you didn't have an arranged marriage, then, Vashti, isn't that what 'you lot' do?

BRIAN

Don't complain about Mark.

Not if you want that consultancy.

VASHTI

Why not?

BRIAN

Because... It'll make you look weak. Not Mark.

Beat

VASHTI

This job is not about saying please and thank you and being nice.

BRIAN

Sometimes, it is.

VASHTI

It's about having standards.

BRIAN

You can't be a perfectionist in a hospital.

A&E

Mark and Rebecca. Mark is busily filling in a form.

MARK

A bullying form.

REBECCA

What?

MARK

I'm filling out a bullying form. I've only got two questions left.

REBECCA

You are *joking*.

Beat

MARK

No, I'm not.

(*He carries on writing.*)

It's amazing how many of these boxes I'm ticking.

'Have they taken aversion to your physical appearance?' I'm going to have to say, 'yes.'

Don't you remember? Vashti said to me 'If you want to be a surgeon, you'd better get rid of the goatee, for a start.'

REBECCA

Well, she had a point.

– Oh, for fuck's sake, Mark, don't be a /twat.

MARK

/Why should I be patronised by someone who isn't even that good?

(*Emily comes up, silently, and starts collecting up some notes.*)

She can't cut. She hasn't got the balls for it.

REBECCA

What have balls got to do with anything?

MARK

She's a crap surgeon, with a crap manner.

REBECCA

Name me one surgeon that *doesn't* have a crap manner. You /included.

MARK

/Listen.

(*He turns to Emily.*)

What do you want to be, surgeon or medic?

EMILY

...Surgeon

MARK

And why do you want to be a surgeon?

EMILY

'Cos...you actually do something. (*She gestures with her hands miming her next few phrases*) Bone's snapped, you *fix* it. You see something bad – you *cut* the badness out. Rather than trying some drugs... standing back... seeing what happens... trying different drugs... That's why I want to be a surgeon, not a medic.

Mark is looking at her.

MARK

You know what surgery's really about?

Slabs of meat. Not people.

You saw this morning. You've got a slab of meat on a table rendered helpless by the anaesthetic. You've got supreme power. They can't fight you.

REBECCA

(*To Emily, apologetically*) This is his way of trying to impress –

MARK

(*Ignoring her*) /And you have to be able to live with what you do to that slab of meat. When you make a hole in the wrong place. Because once you open the skin you're on your own.

(*To Rebecca*)

I've watched Vashti. She's scared when she cuts.

That's why she'll always be a crap surgeon.

EMILY

Well, the surgical reg said that on the rotation here –

MARK

Hold on a second. You're going to apply for the surgical rotation here?

EMILY

I haven't decided yet. My boyfriend's already on it and –

MARK

Your boyfriend?

EMILY

James Ransom. Orthopaedics.

REBECCA

(*Seeing Mark's expression, under her breath*) Give it a rest, Mark.

MARK

(*Sing-song*) Oooohhh... I didn't know 'Handsome Ransom' had a girlfriend.

EMILY

What do you mean, 'Handsome Ransom'?

MARK

Nothing, nothing. (*Drawling*) 'Orthopaedics...' So, your boyfriend's a bone monkey. Does he like playing with lego? (*He looks at her, with ironic wonderment*) God, you don't like me being rude about him, do you? *Very* haughty. Carry on, you were saying?

EMILY

(*Changing her mind*) – Look, I've got to go. I'm meant to be taking these ECGs to Cardiology –

MARK

(*Interrupting her*) How much operating did you do in your last job?

EMILY

Well, I just observed. Three months. Breast.

MARK

Mm. Brrreast...Well, give it a little more time. Try *doing* a few operations that go wrong. Do you know what it's like to be the person who's actually sticking the knife in here? Or here? (*He gestures to two arterial points – in the groin, and near the armpit*) You stick a knife in close to an artery, boy do you know it.

Then you're in tiger country.

(*He looks at her.*)

You're a medic. Not a surgeon. You'll end up in GP land. I give
you six months.

He goes.

CARDIOLOGY

John and Mrs Bracken in a small room together. Mrs Bracken
(Essex accent) is in her early sixties and looks pale and sweaty. John
is taking her pulse.

JOHN

Are you nervous?...

MRS BRACKEN

Why?

JOHN

No, just 'cos your pulse is bounding a bit.

*Emily comes in with some pieces of A4 pink graph paper with a se-
ries of jagged graph lines across them: Mrs Bracken's ECG printouts.*

EMILY

The ECGs.

JOHN

His face is expressionless as he scans the graphs.

(*Under his breath*) Mhm, mhm...fair enough, fair enough...

EMILY

(*Looking over his shoulder, in an undertone*) Quite...um...is it,
saggy inferiorly, isn't it?

JOHN

Mmh.

(*Louder, to Mrs Bracken.*)

So, Mrs Bracken... Mary... first it was just the burning in the throat –

MRS BRACKEN

Yes but put it this way, I'm feeling none too good altogether now.

JOHN

Mmhm. What I want to do, right now, is have another quick listen, and then I'm going to look at your heart myself, my love. If you could lift up your top...

She does so. She is facing out towards the audience. John takes his stethoscope, puts it to the lady's chest, and listens. He does not look at her but his face is cocked out to the audience too. His expression is inscrutable.

Silence. Everyone is still. Finally

JOHN

Right.

(*He gestures to a stretcher couch.*)

If you could just lie down there... and unbutton your top for me, Mary...

She does so.

MRS BRACKEN

What are you going to do?

Emily hovers uncertainly.

JOHN

(*To Emily*) You should stay and watch.

(*He pulls on some gloves, takes a tube of clear jelly-like substance.*)

This might feel a bit cold. What we're doing is called an echocardiogram and on that screen – (*He gestures to a computer screen at the bedside*) – we should be able to get a look at your heart.

(*He puts some jelly on her chest.*)

(*To himself*) ...And see what this is all about.

MRS BRACKEN

Ooh that is cold.

JOHN

Sorry about that.

(*To Emily*) Could you switch off the lights for me?

(*She does so. The computer screen glows in the dark room. John moves a plastic rod over Mrs Bracken's chest. On the screen a black and white, very grainy fuzzy image of the heart and the sound of its beats. The beats do not sound like the typical clichéd sound effect. Amplified, they sound like footsteps far away, echoing down a corridor.*)

There we go... we...

(*The heart bulges in and out of view, shifting and pulsing.*)

...We have to make use of what views we can get. See there's your lungs getting in the way.

MRS BRACKEN

Sorry about that. Shall I move them?

JOHN

Yep, on the shelf over there...

They chuckle. Then, silence, filled with the noise of the heartbeats.

John manipulates the rod, to get a different view.

Emily moves closer, studying the image on the screen.

JOHN

How did you get here today, Mrs Bracken?

MRS BRACKEN

My husband drove me. We live a little bit out, beyond Stamford Bridge, do you know it?

JOHN

I do. Very pretty. I was thinking of buying there.

(*Beat*)

(*Casually*) Where is your husband now?

MRS BRACKEN

In the corridor, poor thing.

(*Beat*)

Where do you live?

JOHN

Islington.

(*A pause while he carries on manipulating the image. Emily sees something in the image and cranes in to look. John has seen it too.*)

(*Abstractedly*) But I want to move...

MRS BRACKEN

Why's that then?

JOHN

Just... not very convenient for work... Bit hectic. Be nice to get away from it all a bit.

(*Beat*)

EMILY

(*In an undertone*) The right atrium.

JOHN

(*Shortly*) Yup.

Pause.

MRS BRACKEN

Your job must tire you out.

JOHN

Sometimes.

Pause.

MRS BRACKEN

Because you're not well at the moment, are you?

(*Beat. John looks at Mrs Bracken directly for the first time.*)

JOHN

What?

MRS BRACKEN

You're not well.

(*Beat*)

I know you're only young, but you've got something wrong with you.

JOHN

Oh dear, what would that be?

MRS BRACKEN

You look tired to death.

JOHN

That's just being a doctor I'm afraid.

(*There is silence again as John continues to probe with the ultra-sound.*)

OK, I think we'd better... Let's just try... (*To Mrs Bracken*) See, the heart is dependent on itself for its own blood supply. It pumps blood into itself. This'll show us whether that's... this'll show us the direction of flow.

(*Beat*)

(*To himself*) It'll show us if there's... turbulent flow.

(*He changes the image on the screen. Now the heart is strikingly rainbow coloured, like a heat-sensitive photograph. Red blending to blue, yellow and green, fanning and flowing.*)

Right.

(*To Emily*) Tamponade.

EMILY

(*Shocked*) Really?

JOHN

Mrs Bracken, there's nothing to panic about, but what's happened is, you've got some...fluid round the heart...see there? (*He indicates on the screen*)

MRS BRACKEN

Fluid round the heart?

JOHN

Yes... just there – (*he indicates again*) – and that's what's causing your problems. And...we need to treat this.

He starts to pack up the probe, strip off his gloves. Switches on the lights.

MRS BRACKEN

Right away?

JOHN

Well... the sooner the better really.

(*He is ready to go.*)

So, I'm going to leave Dr Logan with you while I go and tell the relevant people, and we'll get this sorted out for you in no time.

He starts to leave the room.

MRS BRACKEN

And I just wait here?

JOHN

You just wait here. And take it easy Mrs Bracken. (*To Emily*) You can get started on the notes.

MRS BRACKEN

Well, this is what I call service!

He exits, Emily follows, joins John outside the room. He is busily dialling a number into a phone.

JOHN

Fluid's built up around the heart in the pericardial cavity. You saw how the right atrium was almost completely collapsed in diastole.

EMILY

Shit, so –

JOHN

So the pressure build up could stop the heart beating if we don't get a move on. Yep.

EMILY

Oh my God.

JOHN

No, well done. You went on a hunch and you were right. Now all we have to do (*he gestures to phone*) is wait for 'our man' to answer the bleep.

(*He nods, looks at her.*)

You're good. You listen and you look. And you ask them the right questions.

And that's what it's about.

EMILY

Is it?

JOHN

Yeah. Asking the right questions, but sometimes, just listening...

EMILY

To what?

JOHN

Your gut... your heart... your blood... whatever...

(*Beat*)

You had a feeling about her, didn't you?

Sometimes your body gets there first and tells you. 'There's something wrong here.'

Something you saw out of the corner of your eye and you never knew what it was because your body told you before your brain got there.

When you're walking down a dark street and something tells you to turn around.

He looks at her.

EMILY

What do we do now?

JOHN

We stick a needle in and we let off the fluid before her heart stops beating entirely and she dies. (*He grins*)

Or rather, we bleep our consultant Dr West who will stick in the needle for us when we've told him what's happened. Who should be calling us back right about –

(*The phone rings.*)

– Now. Answering my bleep.

(*The phone rings.*)

You want to pick it up?

(*The phone rings.*)

And have the satisfaction of telling him it wasn't acid reflux or candidiasis of the throat yourself?

(*The phone rings.*)

Go on. You deserve it. Enjoy it.

Have a chat with him. Man to man.

It won't happen that often.

The phone rings. They stare at each other. They are still.

INTERVAL

ACT TWO

THE WARD

Some weeks later.

Vashti is sitting next to a bed. In the bed is a middle-aged Indian lady, who speaks a mixture of Hindi (in bold) and English (in a strong Indian accent). After a brief pause:

BINDU

Vo tumse pyaar karta hai, aur vo tumhe bohot yaad karta hai. Von tumharaj intasaar karega. Tumhare seeva aur koyee nahee hoga. Manlo ooski baat, behta.... ['He loves you and he misses you – he's going to wait until you see sense and he knows you will eventually – he says there'll never be anyone else]

VASHTI

Look, Jaspreed has obviously been bending your ear, but I've had a long time to think it over, and I'm not going to change my mind. We got married. We also got divorced. For a reason.

BINDU

Behta, darad maan mah hota hai – [You're upset because –]

VASHTI

No. I'm not upset about it anymore. Mind over matter.

Can we talk about you now, please?

(*Beat*)

Is everything all set for tomorrow?

BINDU

Yes. Meve khyalse jo meva 'operation' karega ooska naam 'Mr Milward' hai. ['Apparently the doctor who's going to do me is called... 'Mr Milward'... at least I think that's what they said – it was something like that.']

VASHTI

Oh right, Milward. Well, he'll do a good job. Hopefully.

BINDU

They took some bits of blood... testing I think –

VASHTI

Look, just speak Hindi will you? It's fine.

Beat.

BINDU

Vashti, mai bohot pareshan hoon. ['Vashti, I'm worried about this operation...] Things go wrong...you know they do –

VASHTI

(*Interrupting*) Oh God, Bindu. I've told you zillions of times. It'll be very simple. Very straightforward. Very routine. It'll be over before you can –

BINDU

Too samajti nahi hai. Ye log toomhara badaan nahi kaat ne vale. ['You don't understand, Vashti – you're not the one going in there and being chopped open –']

VASHTI

(*Interrupting*) The only way to sort out the pain is to have it taken out. You've been dithering about this for – I know you're scared of hospitals but honestly, you couldn't have chosen a simpler operation. Look. I'll explain it to you. You'll be under a *general anaesthetic.* I know it sounds mad but pain is perception... **Darad maan me hota hai...** ['Pain is perception'] ...do you see what I'm saying?

(*Bindu makes to disagree but Vashti is there first*) Also, Bindu, I got you bumped up the list... **Aapke leeye maine bohot kaushish kee hai...** ['I pulled strings left right and centre for you'] ...You went on and on about the pain, if you pull out now you won't get done for months.

Beat

BINDU

Aaccha, toom jaantee ho! ['I suppose you're the expert.']

VASHTI

Exactly. I am. I am the expert. So just lie back, and enjoy it. What time are they doing you?

BINDU

8.30.

VASHTI

Good. You're first on the list, everyone'll be fresh, and you won't be cancelled.

(*Beat*)

Honestly, darling, take it from me. You're doing the right thing.

BINDU

Vashti, too mooje milne aarogee na operation ke baad? ['Will you come and see me when it's over?']

VASHTI

Of course I will, *Massi*. When you come round. Oh God, no, I can't. I'm going to a conference. And preparing for my interview. It'll have to be the day after, in the evening.

But you're going to be fine, *Massi*.

BINDU

God willing.

VASHTI

Forget about *him*. *I'll* be looking out for you.

(*She gets up.*)

That's what I'm here for, darling.

EMILY'S ROOM

This is a typical on-site hospital on-call room. Small, Spartan. A narrow bed and not much else. Emily is finishing a conversation on her mobile phone. There is something different about her, dispirited.

EMILY

Mum, I can't talk. I can't think about it. I'm too tired.

(*Pause*)

Well why don't you tell *him* that?

(*Pause*)

Mum –

(*Pause*)

I don't know!

I don't know what it 'means'. I'm not psychic.

Why don't you just talk to each other for once?

(*Pause*)

No, *you* talk to *him*.

I don't know because I wasn't there. So it's pointless asking me –

(*Beat*)

There's nothing 'wrong' with me.

Mum, I'm standing here getting a brain tumour. I'll speak to you tomorrow when I can think straight.

She listens for a beat, then puts the phone down, obviously in the

middle of the other person's sentence. It immediately rings again.
She throws herself flat on the bed, lets it ring, doesn't pick up.

There is a knock at the door. Emily goes to it, opens it. James
comes in.

EMILY

Shit! ...*Shit!* What are you doing here?

(*They hug. Emily is delighted.*)

I thought you were on call.

JAMES

I am. A&E is dead. I'm going to catch some kip. With you. Because you're not in Brighton anymore, you're not a two hour drive away, you're right here where I can get you, so they can bloody well bleep me if they need me.

God, it's good to see you.

(*They kiss. He looks around the room.*)

That fucking bed.

EMILY

I know.

JAMES

Three months here and you still haven't done anything about it. Screwed my back. (*He throws himself on to her bed, prods around behind him*) It isn't a bed. It's a fucking portcullis. (*He lies back, gingerly.*)

Still, better than nothing.

Come here.

(*He squints at her.*)

You look gorgeous.

(*She is wiping her makeup off with a small rag.*)

Is that a swab?!

EMILY

They're perfect for taking makeup off.

JAMES

Ingenious use of hospital resources.

(*She walks over, looks down at him, but doesn't get on the bed.*)

You're upside down.

Please don't spit on me.

(*Pause*)

So tell me.

EMILY

What?

JAMES

Everything. Tell me about your day.

EMILY

My mum's been bending my ear again... *family*. And – caught a meningococcal septicaemia.

JAMES

Good *call*. What happened?

EMILY

(*She moves away from him*) Girl complaining of flu-like symptoms. The reg wasn't having any of it because she'd been in two days before with a sore throat, he thought she was a Munch's. He said what she needed was a boot up the arse.

JAMES

'A leather suppository.'

EMILY

Exactly. Well it wasn't barn door, she just had a headache, not photophobic, but then I had a look at her ankle and she'd got a little red spot that didn't blanch when I pressed it... And the lab called back six hours later and said... they'd grown gram negative diplococci from her blood cultures.

JAMES

Fucking hell. You tell the reg?

EMILY

Yeah.

JAMES

And?

EMILY

...I feel like shit.

JAMES

Why? That's great. Shows you've got great hunches.

EMILY

No, I just see the worst all the time. (*Comes slowly over to him*) I wish I hadn't been right about that girl.

JAMES

Why?

EMILY

Because then I wouldn't mind that I'd nearly sent her home without double-checking.

JAMES

But you did double-check.

EMILY

Because I'm an obsessive compulsive. Did I check the notes. Did I check the bloods. It feels like there's no space left in my head.

It doesn't help when I get proved right.

JAMES

The best docs are OCD, you know that.

EMILY

...(*This is hard for her to say*) ...*And* I fucking missed something.

JAMES

What?

EMILY

This old guy. Handed on to me at the end of the afternoon, twenty minutes away from breaching, Bed manager was whipping my arse to get him onto the ward, I kept getting bleeps telling me to hurry up, *everyone* was hassling me to hand him over. And just as I did, I saw his ECGs upside-down in his notes, I thought 'Hang on' but it was too late, they'd gone.

They showed that he'd had a heart attack. He'd broken his hip and while he'd been stuck on the floor he'd had a heart attack.

JAMES

Doesn't make any difference. He'd already had the heart attack.

EMILY

I've made my first mistake.

JAMES

Look. You're in A&E, you make the first, basic decision – take them in or send them away. Anything else and you're wasting time. Say you get an aneurysm – they can pop off any minute to the great Sainsbury's in the sky. Or say you have to lead an arrest –

EMILY

Thanks for these merry little tales, but I haven't had to yet.

JAMES

But it's only a matter of time. And when it happens, you'll be the *most* inexperienced person there, but they'll all be looking at you to tell them what to do, and *everyone*'ll see, straightaway, whether you're any good or not. Then you'll *have* to make quick decisions.

EMILY

I know! But it's...these bloody decisions all the time.

I can feel them all still.

JAMES

Feel them?

Beat

EMILY

On my back...

Do you think the job... makes us sick?

Beat

JAMES

This bit's the worst, Em. I drank a lot in my first A&E job. You last this, you'll be OK.

EMILY

One day, I really *will* fuck up.

JAMES

No. *Every* day, you will fuck up. And if *you* don't, the next person'll fuck up for you. (*Ironically*) 'Teamwork.' That's what it's all about.

Beat

EMILY

Someone is going to die...

JAMES

Everyone's going to die...

They kiss. Beat.

EMILY

Is there someone else?

Beat

JAMES

Where did that come from?

Beat

EMILY

We're all right?

JAMES

Yes, we're all right. Why?

Why are you looking at me like that?

EMILY

Why are *you* looking at me like that?

JAMES

Like what?

EMILY

Talk to me.

JAMES

(*Tenderly*) I am talking to you... Now shut up. Jesus.

(*He kisses her. Beat. James sits up, starts to take her top off. Quietly, as if he is telling her a story.*)

When you want to find out what's going on... there are *lots* of things you can do...

(*He illustrates as he undresses her.*)

First of all you look at what's in front of you...

And then you listen... to what they say to you...

And then you feel... the bit they say is hurting...

(*He puts his hand to her shoulders.*)

And see if you can feel anything...

And you might listen to their chest... or to their heart...

And if they're a little kid... you ask them lots of questions.

EMILY

Like what?

JAMES

Like what their favourite food is... the name of their art teacher... because sometimes the answers to the questions are not important... it's what they do while they're thinking about them... They forget when they're meant to say ouch... (*He touches her*) ...and you find out where it really hurts...

And there are lots and lots and lots of tests you can do...

But never forget... to listen to your gut.

He puts his hand on her stomach.

EMILY

(*Playing along*) My stomach?

JAMES

Yes. Because the gut's all covered by these nerves... that are like...the wiring... left over from the old, primitive nervous system... from a long time ago, from before we had a brain... like in earthworms, and flies...

...and it's where you feel happy and where you feel sad.

EMILY

(*Drily*) And what about listening to your brain?

JAMES

Well your brain can control a lot... like it can make my finger wiggle... (*He wiggles one finger*) ...but it can't control what you feel down here... Because there's a different sort of brain down there... and all those primitive things you can't control... like breathing... or feeling angry... or just feeling... it's the gut brain that's controlling them. And that's why you should listen to it. Because you can't control it.

They kiss.

THE MESS

Night. John sits in the mess, staring into space. He has a dressing on his neck. The lights are off. The room is lit only by the TV, which is on mute. John ignores it. He slowly starts to collect his belongings. He sits, riffling through his bag. Brian comes in, sees John. Stops. Watches him but doesn't say anything. John, sensing something, turns around, sees Brian.

JOHN

Hey.

BRIAN

Hey. What are you sitting in the dark for?

JOHN

Dunno. Well, bit of a day.

(*He heaves a sigh. Hums for a second.*)

Can't get rid of it. (*He hums again*) Had it on the brain all day.

Beat

BRIAN

I chased your biopsy for you. It's come back.

JOHN

Already? My biopsy? No way!

BRIAN

Yeah.

JOHN

(*Getting up*) Shit, man! Thanks. How come –

BRIAN

I knew you wouldn't, so I did.

JOHN

Hope they didn't give you a hard time, the lab?

BRIAN

No no. They owe me, anyway. I just gave them a friendly prod. spoke to Bob at the end of the MDT. Turned out Prof Kroll was dealing with it.

JOHN

Well no wonder. You know what he's like.

BRIAN

Yeah.

JOHN

Fills you with a perfectly healthy, natural desire –

BRIAN

– to kill him.

They laugh. Beat. John rubs his neck, involuntarily.

JOHN

What's the story?

BRIAN

Well, really you need to talk to Prof. Kroll. Not me.

I just wanted to let you know that the results were back.

JOHN

Why?

(*Suddenly John turns, switches on the lights. They flicker on. Both men blink in the sudden neon light. A pause.*)

You're doing it. You're giving me that look.

BRIAN

What look?

JOHN

The *look.*

(*Beat*)

My cells are ugly.

BRIAN

John... I don't want to be the one to talk you through it now. I just wanted to tell you that I chased the results and they're back. You need to talk to them. Plus, you know that there are limits to what you can deduce from the biopsy. It's difficult to say exactly... what it shows.

JOHN

Oh, please, don't talk to me like that.

BRIAN

Like what.

JOHN

Like I'm one of *them*.

(*Beat*)

I dreamt about my cells. There were too many of them, purples and blues.

Tell me what they looked like.

BRIAN

I can't tell you because I didn't look at them.

(*Beat*)

The histologists said that the cells didn't look entirely... normal. No.

(*Beat*)

JOHN

OK... OK.

Beat

BRIAN

Grade two.

JOHN

Thanks.

Beat. He sits down.

BRIAN

You don't know –

JOHN

So this thing in my neck, that's been sitting there for three months, is a lymphoma. Yes. I do know that.

What do you think I should do?

BRIAN

Oh, Christ, John... You're a doctor. You know you shouldn't be asking me –

JOHN

Yes; because this shouldn't be happening to me!

I spend my life watching other people get sick and die. And it's a *shit life.*

I've paid my dues, haven't I?

Beat

BRIAN

You know that this could be nothing.

JOHN

But that's not what I'm getting from you.

(*Beat*)

I need you to tell me what to do. You're the doctor now.

Beat.

BRIAN

Get it all cut out.

JOHN

Get it all cut out.

BRIAN

Yes.

JOHN

And hope for the best.

John is still, staring ahead of him. Softly, he starts to hum – the same tune – again.

ACT THREE

A&E

Emily stands, on her own. She is reading, aloud, from the Oxford Medical Handbook.

EMILY

'Is your pain sharp or dull? Sharp like a knife, or dull and crushing?' Patients often avoid using the word "pain"... "wind", "tightening", "burning", or "a lump in the throat" may be used... Symptoms are often half-formed, and it is our role to give them a local habitation and a name. Be as vague in your questioning as your patient is in his answers... A patient came to one of us saying 'last night I dreamt I had a pain in my chest...'

(*She puts her hand on her chest.*)

'...Now I've woken up, and I'm not so sure. Have I got a chest pain, doctor?'

Then, she goes to sit with an old lady, GILLIAN who is sitting up on a bed. There is a tight, blood-stained bandage on her head. Her husband stands next to her.

EMILY

I'm *sorry* you had such a long wait... She's definitely going to need stitches from what you've told me – it's a long gash, is it?

HUSBAND

Oh yes. Very long. (*He gestures vaguely*) I couldn't look at it. Flapping away from the... you can actually see her... the skull underneath...

EMILY

Well... you *have* been in the wars...

HUSBAND

...If she's hurt, I'm hurt. It's as simple as that.

Emily makes a note.

EMILY

And she can usually verbalise normally... (*Emily pats her arm*)... Sorry to talk about you... I *know* you can ...

GILLIAN

– Yes, yes! –

EMILY

I just have to ask.

HUSBAND

Oh yes. Yes, absolutely.

EMILY

But at the moment she can *only* say yes and no.

GILLIAN

Yes.

EMILY

Right. Well... I think I'm going to test your reflexes, Gillian, before we do anything else...

(*She does so, knocking on her knees, shining a torch into her eyes. She scratches the soles of the old lady's feet with a stick. Gillian, not expecting this, is slightly distressed.*)

Sorry, we're being *mean* to you, aren't we.

(*Emily stops, carefully replaces, again, one of her slippers which has fallen off her foot.*)

OK. (*Talking directly to Gillian*) Let's just stick with yeses and nos for the moment, otherwise I think it's going to be a bit traumatic for you.

Do you feel sick, Gillian?

GILLIAN

No.

HUSBAND

She was sick once, just a little bit. In the ambulance.

EMILY

Any blood in the vomit?

HUSBAND

I don't know. I didn't really look.

GILLIAN

No.

EMILY

OK.

(*To Gillian*) Do you feel dizzy?

GILLIAN

No.

EMILY

Right.

(*Beat*)

Gillian. Is the main thing that's worrying you your speech?

GILLIAN

(*Straining to find words*) Yes. Yes. Yes. (*She is upset*)

EMILY

OK, Gillian. (*She puts her hand on her arm*) Well don't worry, because generally in cases like this, the speech *is* recovered, it just takes a little time.

HUSBAND

What's happened? Is it her heart?

EMILY

No, it's not her heart, I'm... pretty sure what's happened is that Gillian has actually had a little stroke, and that's why she fell.

HUSBAND

How do you know?

EMILY

I don't know, I just... I'm making a guess here, but I think as a result of this particular little stroke she's got what we call 'expressive dysphasia', which is when you know what to say but you can't say it, you can't...

Sorry, I'm not being very clear. It's... a little breakdown in communication within your own brain. Like a short circuit. (*To Gillian*) But, the brain is very good at adapting, so the chances are, with any luck, you will recover your speech.

GILLIAN

Yes.

(*Rebecca has come up and hears what Emily says next.*)

EMILY

Now, what I'm going to do first, is refer you to a team. And then the team will take a scan so we know better what's going on. Any questions?

HUSBAND

No. Thank you very much, doctor.

GILLIAN

Yes.

HUSBAND

Just make my beautiful wife well again.

Beat

EMILY

Yes.

Gillian is wheeled off by a nurse. Emily moves straight to a phone. Rebecca watches her.

REBECCA

Aren't you going to get her a scan before you refer her? You're doing it in the wrong order.

EMILY

No, she's about to breach and the nurses are going mental at me, I'm going to get her on a team first. (*In response to her look*) What?

REBECCA

No, just, if you think you can get her accepted by the medics without a scan, good luck to you.

EMILY

But she's about to breach.

REBECCA

Yeah, you're welcome to go and get shouted at. But if you think it'll work you're a brave woman is all I can say.

EMILY

(*An edge to her voice*) So I'll refer her to the surgeons.

REBECCA

(*With some derision*) The *surgeons* won't take her!

EMILY

Why not?

REBECCA

Because she's had a stroke. She automatically goes to the medics.

EMILY

But she needs to be stitched. Look, the medics need to deal with the stroke. The surgeons need to stitch her. One of the teams will take her, they've both got reason to.

REBECCA

And that's exactly why they won't.

(*Emily picks up a phone, starts dialling*)

Fine, go ahead, try your luck.

EMILY

Thanks, I will.

THE WARD

Vashti stands by Bindu's bedside. Bindu looks terrible. Her eyes are shut, her face is sweaty. Every now and again she twitches from one side to the other. Vashti looks at her, feels her forehead. Goes to the end of the bed, looks at the 'obs' – the chart of Bindu's temperature, blood pressure etc. She doesn't like the look of them. Looks at Bindu again. A nurse drifts by and Vashti moves away to intercept him

VASHTI

Hi.

(*The nurse looks like he's going to carry on going.*)

Hello, nurse –

NURSE

Sorry. Can I help you?

VASHTI

Yes. Can you fill me in on what's been happening to my aunt?

NURSE

Your aunt?

VASHTI

(*Pointing*) My aunt. Over there. Mrs Mehta.

Beat

NURSE

Oh right, Mrs Mehta. What would you like to know, exactly?

VASHTI

She's not conscious, she's sweaty, she's tossing and turning, and if you ask me, she looks peritonitic. So what I want to know is, what's going on? And when was the last time she was seen by a doctor?

Beat

NURSE

Well, she had an operation a couple of days ago –

VASHTI

On her gall bladder, I know. And?

NURSE

I know she was in some pain, afterwards, and she was prescribed morphine by the doctor to help alleviate it.

VASHTI

And?

NURSE

And it seems as though – the doctors think that she may be morphine sensitive, which is why she's –

VASHTI

No. This is not the picture of someone who is 'morphine sensitive.'

(*She goes to the bedside, picks up the drain which is snaking out from underneath the covers.*)

Has she been seen today?

NURSE

My shift has only just started so –

VASHTI

Has she been seen today?

NURSE

Yes. But I don't know exactly when because –

VASHTI

What was she like this morning? Was she like this? How long has this been going on for? Since the operation? Has she deteriorated?

NURSE

I'm afraid I can't tell you any of that. Not without looking at the notes.

VASHTI

Why not?

NURSE

(*His tone hardening*) Because, as I said, my shift's only just started. And I've had two days off.

 Beat

VASHTI

So is there someone who *can* tell me? (*Before he has time to answer, referring to the drain*) Has anyone sent this off for bile?

(*The nurse looks blank. As if to a five year old*) If the surgeons have made a hole in the wrong place then bile will be leaking out into her abdomen.

Which would not be a good thing.

 Beat

NURSE

Would you like to speak to a doctor?

VASHTI

Yes. I would.

James comes up. He is jovial.

JAMES

Hey, Vashti! (*He glances at his watch*) What are you doing here? You don't have any patients on this ward.

The nurse takes the opportunity of this distraction to make his escape.

VASHTI

I came to see my aunt.

JAMES

Your aunt? I didn't know you had a relly in.

VASHTI

I know, not many people did. Mrs Mehta. (*She gestures down at the bed, right next to them*)

JAMES

(*Digesting this, sobering up*) Oh. Right.

(*Beat*)

They just bleeped me and asked me to come up from A&E –

VASHTI

Yes. It was me who asked them to bleep you.

JAMES

Right.

Beat

VASHTI

What's going on? She looks like shit.

(*Beat. A realisation.*)

I can't believe this is happening.

JAMES

Yeah. Um, they think it might be that she's morphine sensitive.

VASHTI

Oh for God's sake, James. What is all this 'morphine sensitive' crap? (*She flicks through the chart on the end of the bed*) My aunt's febrile, her blood pressure's in her boots – this is not someone who's sensitive to morphine. This is someone who is septic.

JAMES

You don't know that.

VASHTI

What happened when Milward operated on her?

(*Beat*)

Oh Jesus.

JAMES

I don't know, I wasn't there.

VASHTI

He's made a hole, hasn't he.

JAMES

I don't know. I started a week of shifts in A&E the day of her operation.

Beat

VASHTI

James, please –

JAMES

Vashti –

VASHTI

I want to see the operating notes.

JAMES

...Vashti, I can't.

VASHTI

Yes, you can. I work here, I'm your senior, I'm asking you to get me the notes.

Beat

JAMES

I can't get you the notes.

VASHTI

Why not.

JAMES

Because at this moment in time, you're not a doctor.

VASHTI

What am I then?

JAMES

A relative.

A&E: DOCTORS' STATION

Emily and Mark, mid-argument.

MARK

Because it's not a case for the surgeons. That's why. She needs to be seen by the medics.

EMILY

Mark, it's seven o'clock, she came in at *three-thirty*, she's got a massive laceration, at the very least she needs to be stitched up –

MARK

So why don't you stitch her then?

EMILY

Because this is too big for me to stitch! It's from here to here, it's like she's been scalped. I've never stitched anything that big before, I don't know what stitches to use, if I need to shave her, and I'm nervous of taking the compression bandage off –

MARK

You mean you haven't even *examined* the lac yet, and you want me to stitch it up for you? (*He laughs*) I don't believe this.

EMILY

I didn't want her to start hosing blood everywhere.

MARK

You saying you're scared of blood?

EMILY

I can't do it, it's too big for me to manage on my own, and she's about to breach! This is your *job*! – Why have you got such a problem with me?

MARK

Why do you think everything's about you?

EMILY

Let me get this straight. Are you or are you not going to help?

MARK

I'm not going to take this as a referral.

EMILY

Why *not?*

MARK

(*Getting up*) Because I've got an appendectomy to do and I want to do that instead. I don't want to be stuck here stitching for hours and miss going to theatre. Do it and stop being such a baby. It's just a flap of skin.

EMILY

And real men go to theatre and do appendixes. Very impressive.

MARK

You want to be a surgeon – *stitch* it.

EMILY

OK, I will. (*She dials in a phone*) Thanks. Thanks, Mark, for being so delightful. Full marks, Mark. Sorry you're on your period.

MARK

Christ, you think everyone's in love with you, don't you?

EMILY

What?

MARK

Well, I'm not in love with you −

EMILY

No, you're in love with *yourself*, you wanker, I can't believe you /just −

MARK

(*He is going*) − /Just because you've got a pair of tits, doesn't mean you get whatever you want.

Someone has picked up at the other end of Emily's phone so all she can do is glare at Mark as he goes.

EMILY

(*Containing herself with some effort*) − Hi. Is that the medical SHO on call?

Yes, I've got a patient I'd like to refer to the medics. 75-year-old lady, suffered a bang to the head, large scalp laceration, severe expressive dysphasia, query haemorrhagic stroke.

What?

Sorry, but this is just stupid.

(*Rebecca comes up, starts writing notes.*)

(*Presto*) Look. I'd *love* to get her a CT scan but by the time I've got a CT scan she will have breached her wait time. Which is why I'm ringing you. If you won't take her *without* a scan how on earth am I meant to − ?

(*Ironically*) Fine.

No, thank you very much.

No. I *will* talk to my consultant.

(*She puts the phone down, turns on Rebecca.*)

For *fuck's* sake. The medics won't take her, the surgeons won't take her, we *know* what's wrong with her, but the lady is sitting there, gradually losing blood and becoming unstable, while I go round in circles, all because one department won't communicate with another.

And all anyone will say is 'no.' Not 'yes': 'No. No. No.'

REBECCA

Expressive dysphasia. Welcome to A&E.

THE WARD

Lakshmi stands, looking at a file. Vashti stands with her, keeping an eye out − this is illicit.

LAKSHMI

...These notes are incomplete.

VASHTI

Are you sure?

LAKSHMI

Well, there's nothing in here really.

She peers at them again.

VASHTI

I need to sit down.

(*She puts her head in her hands.*)

My hands... I'm tingling all over.

LAKSHMI

Who wrote them? The reg would have written them, wouldn't he?

(*They both look at the notes again.*)

Oh. That explains it.
Yep.

VASHTI

Milward.

LAKSHMI

– Wrote them himself.

Beat

Well, that's pretty simple. You need to get hold of him.

A&E

Emily and James at the coffee point.

JAMES

I bet you gave everyone exactly the same spiel. Didn't you.

EMILY

I can't remember anymore. My head hurts.

JAMES

Everyone spins. Buff, turf, bounce. It's the first thing you learn in Casualty. How many different ways are there of telling the truth? Loads. Just know who you're talking to, and sell them the case.

EMILY

This job isn't about giving a performance.

JAMES

Yes, it is.

EMILY

You could have stitched her.

JAMES

I was busy.

EMILY

Arsing about with Rebecca.

JAMES

We weren't arsing /about.

EMILY

/Bullshit, I heard her laugh down the phone.

She's got thick ankles, by the way. In case you hadn't noticed. That's why she always wears boots. (*She flicks her hair*) 'Oh, I'm Re*becca*.'

JAMES

(*His face is expressionless*) That is not attractive.

EMILY

I don't care.

It wouldn't have made any difference *what* I said to Mark. He's been a wanker to me ever since I said I was applying for the surgical rotation here. And right now, you're being a wanker too.

JAMES

So you are going to apply?

EMILY

Yes! I am going to apply!

(*Beat*)

You don't want me to either, do you? Because you don't like us working in the same hospital.

JAMES

Look, I haven't got time for this. My shift finishes at nine. And your shift finishes at nine as well. Hand her over and get out of here.

EMILY

Please. You've got half an hour left.

JAMES

I'm meeting my consultant for a drink.

Beat

EMILY

Your consultant? Tonight?

JAMES

Yes. (*Looking at her expression*) ...Oh for Christ's sake, what *is* this?

EMILY

I don't know.

How many different ways are there of telling the truth?

JAMES

Oh, fuck this, Emily, I can't believe you're giving me grief when I haven't seen you properly for weeks because you're *always* staying late, sorting *crap* – well this is *me* doing *my* job for a change, this is me doing *my* overtime, how does it feel? Do you think I *want* to go for a drink with him now? It's what you have to do. Unspoken overtime. That's how the NHS is run. On (*he makes the inverted commas in the air*) 'goodwill.'

EMILY

Like our relationship.

(*Beat*)

JAMES

OK, why don't you do this for me? Hand the woman on to the night team, and leave at nine o'clock, when you're supposed to. With me.

EMILY

I can't.

JAMES

You can, and I'm asking you to.

Pause

EMILY

I can't. I need to do this.

JAMES

And when it comes down to you, that's it. 'No compromise.'

EMILY

You're not on my side anymore.

JAMES

And you're not on mine.

(*Beat*)

You don't get it, do you?

You can give and give and give. And this place will take and take and take. From the lazy shitty nurses to the administrative fuck-ups down to the contract cleaners that don't clean. It's a massive juggernaut riddled with vested interests and inertia and filth and it will fuck you in the arse. You don't get paid more if you work more and you don't get paid less if you work less so work less. Work less. Save yourself. You think you're going to survive on the feelgood factor? This is the Soviet Union. *There isn't enough NHS.* There isn't enough me. I've missed weddings, parties, life events and so have you, I've given my pound of flesh without any regard for my own health and happiness, I've destroyed and suppressed what's important to me, at least give me a career out of it. I won't by staying late. I might by having a drink with my consultant.

I'm out of here. I'm not doing any more unpaid work for the NHS than I have to already.

He goes. She watches him go.

The orthopaedic reg walks hurriedly past.

REG

Oh, you get to hate the noise of that printer. Means there's another one coming.

BRIAN

(*Crossing in opposite direction*) I'm clocking off. Night shift can deal with it.

Gradually, Emily is surrounded by the chaos of A&E as the night shift begins, some doctors packing up to leave, others arriving to start work.

MARK

(*Putting on his white coat*)

Don't you hate it when it starts getting dark at 4 o'clock?

REBECCA

Seen the one in 7? Yuk.

REG

Should have seen his chest X-Ray. It was like – (*Blows raspberry*)

BRIAN

What's he got?

JOHN

He's got fat, that's what he's got. I needed three hands to do the

ECG, two to get one boob out of the /way.

BRIAN

/You know someone's just laid concrete down between resuss and theatre? It's still wet. Quick, go and write your name in it and let's hope we don't get any emergencies in the next three hours.

MARK

(*Grimacing*) Sister, there's an awful smell in here. Is someone going to clean it up?

JAMES

(*Putting on coat, to leave*) You *do* know him because you diagnosed him, mate.

MARK

(*Looking at notes*) Oh! He's not called Ernest at all. He's called /Geoffrey.

REBECCA

(*Putting phone down with a crash*) /Our consultant does not think he's perforated. From the other end of his telephone.

MARK

So where do we put him? Clinical decisions unit?

JAMES

Clinical Dumping Unit, yeah. I'm out of here.

He leaves. The noise of the crash call rings out, drowning out everything else... And persists...

A&E RESUSS

Emily stands in A&E resuss. There are two empty A&E trolleys. She is nervous. Mark walks by, Emily turns and walks into him. There is a moment of inadvertent embrace.

MARK

Whoops! Hey! Sorry.

Oh, it's you.

(*Then he looks at her properly, double-taking.*)

Hey, are you OK? You look *rough.*

EMILY

Thanks. Haven't had much sleep.

I've got a cardiac arrest coming. And I've got to lead it.

MARK

(*Looks at her a moment, gauging, then*) – Oh, I see. First time.

EMILY

Yeah. And it's a 24-year-old girl.

MARK

Shit. Where's the A&E reg?

EMILY

In CT.

MARK

Oh, the doughnut of death.

EMILY

Yeah, with a polytrauma who's in VF arrest and they've got no kit. Why do these things always happen in threes? Why aren't there more of us?

MARK

Because that's the way it is.

(*Beat. The next thing is difficult for him to say.*)

Listen, I'm sorry.

EMILY

What?

MARK

(*He is embarrassed*) The... old lady. Scalp lac. Yesterday.

I don't know why I said all that stuff. It just came out.

EMILY

... Oh that...

Feels like ages ago. I haven't really been to bed.

MARK

I don't know why... I was being a prick. I'm sorry.

EMILY

That's OK. My boyfriend was exactly the same. It's fine.

I've got an arrest to lead. How long did they say again? Over the bat phone?

MARK

Don't know, I didn't hear yours, I was listening for mine. Got a trauma call coming in.

...Who took your old lady in the end?

EMILY

The medics. Got my consultant to ring up and kick ass.

MARK

So who stitched her?

EMILY

I don't know and I don't care, right now.

(*Beat*)

I'm kind of... losing patience... with the patients... do you know what I mean?

MARK

Let me at least buy you a drink or something.

But Emily is looking at the trolley again, nervously.

EMILY

Can you think of anything I might need that we don't have?

MARK

...Adrenalin? That always takes ages to find.

EMILY

Got some right here.

MARK

You'll be fine.

EMILY

But where *is* everyone? I've got no *team*.

Mark is putting on a green plastic apron. More of his team are now turning up, also putting on green plastic aprons.

MARK

Do you want me to get the nurse to put out another crash call?

Emily is trying to leaf through 'the cheese and onion'.

EMILY

Fucking hands are shaking.

The intercom from inside the ambulance, that is relayed to resuss, goes off. Emily jumps.

INTERCOM

(*Scratchily*) Cardiac arrest 24-year-old female

...down time 15 minutes

...CPR last 10 minutes

...ETA two minutes.

MARK

There's your girl. Two minutes.

EMILY

So where the hell's –

Mark stops a passing nurse.

MARK

(*Authoritatively*) Excuse me. Could you put out another crash call? Cardiac arrest's going to be here in two minutes, she still hasn't got an anaesthetist.

NURSE

(*Moving swiftly off*) OK.

Rebecca arrives. The girls are noticeably cool but professional with each other.

REBECCA

Hi. Not here yet?

EMILY

No. Two minutes.

REBECCA

Right. You leading it?

EMILY

Yes.

REBECCA

Have we got everything?

EMILY

Everything apart from a team, yes.

A tense pause. They are at a loss. There is nothing they can do. Emily looks at her watch again. The bells of the crash call ring out. The intercom goes off again.

INTERCOM

Trauma

...35-year-old man

...fallen 30 feet off a building site

...suspected multiple fractures

...Estimated time of arrival two minutes, two minutes.

...Over.

MARK

That's mine. Two minutes as well. Here we go. So we've got a double whammy, they're going to hit us at *exactly* the same time. (*Brightly*) That's nice. 30 feet. Fuck. Wonder what sort of state he'll be in.

You'll be fine.

EMILY

Thanks.

Mark goes over to the rest of his team, who have now all drifted in, and are assembling around the furthest empty bed. James is there. They are all doing up their green plastic aprons. Their reg addresses them, confidently.

SURGICAL REG

Alright guys... hey Mark... Missed you last night, where were you?

MARK

Turning over a new leaf.

REG

Not like you. (*To James, next to her*) Got the grey venflons?

JAMES

Yep. Got messy, did it?

REG

Just a bit. Ended up at Po Na Na's.

JAMES

(*Laughing*) Nuff said.

REG

I don't remember getting home. Alright guys...

They start to align themselves around the bed. Emily and Rebecca stand by their bed. The reg looks at her watch.

MARK

What was he doing up a ladder at (*He looks at his watch*) two in the morning, anyway?

REG

Well, he's either a fireman or a burglar.

MARK

Or very keen to fix his Sky dish.

JAMES

How long have we got?

REG

(*Looking at her watch again*) 'Bout a minute and a half?

Everyone glances at their watches. Suddenly, there is relative silence. While people are not entirely still, they don't seem to feel like talking. The silence lasts for about ten seconds, at which point the anaesthetist comes hurriedly in, tying a cap on.

ANAESTHETIST

Hi. Not here yet?

EMILY

(*She is very relieved*) Oh great, you're here. (*Introducing herself*) Emily. Two minutes. Less. Minute and a half.

ANAESTHETIST

(*Gesturing with his head at the surgical team in their aprons*) Why all the Orthopods?

EMILY

Trauma call.

(*A nurse has come in shortly after the anaesthetist and positioned herself at Emily's bed.*)

Hi.

NURSE

Hi.

Beat. Emily looks at her watch, looks around at her 'team'.

EMILY

Sorry – but – is this all the team we're going to get?

NURSE

Looks like it. There's been another cardiac arrest over in CCU and they're busy with that. The Cardiology reg'll head over here soon as he can.

ANAESTHETIST

So who's going to be leading this?

EMILY

I am.

Beat

NURSE

How long did they say?

EMILY

(*Looking at her watch*) About a minute, now.

There is another, short silence. Everyone looks at their watches. The groups around both beds are now simply waiting.

REG

(*To Mark*)

See you got rid of the goatee, Marco.

MARK

Yeah.

JAMES

Now you just need to get a girlfriend.

MARK

Yeah, yeah, yeah.

Both groups now lapse into silence. Ten seconds. The anaesthetist and the reg have both adopted the same pose – head down, arms folded – and one by one, everyone else unconsciously adopts the same stance.

Suddenly an approaching siren is heard. Everyone rouses themselves. Then there is commotion outside resuss. Sound of doors opening and banging shut, muffled instructions. The teams hover at their beds, waiting to see who it will be for. Finally an ambulance crew manoeuvres a stretcher in through the double doors. The second they are through the Paramedic is talking.

PARAMEDIC

35-year-old man, fallen 30 feet off scaffolding,

ANAESTHETIST

Us?

NURSE

(*Shaking her head*) Surgeons.

Suddenly, with the paramedics and the stretcher, the room feels full of people. Everyone, as if choreographed, makes way for the stretcher, carried in by two ambulance men. There is something balletic, stylised, about the way the surgeons move as a team. Emily's 'team' simply watch, dispassionately.

REG

OK... great...

PARAMEDIC

Suspected multiple fractures...

(*The surgical team are all arranging themselves in a line down each side of the stretcher. The stretcher is manoeuvred until it is by the bed. The man is in a spinal board and neck brace.*)

GCS of 15.

The Reg swiftly checks A B C – airway, breathing and circulation. This should take twenty seconds.

REG

(*Speaking loudly, clearly*) Hello, sir, can you hear me?

MAN

Yes.

REG

Please don't try to nod your head. We're going to ask you where it hurts in a minute and I don't want you to nod or shake, just say yes or no. OK?

MAN

...Yes.

REG

(*She has positioned herself at the man's head*) Very good, OK, sir... What we're going to do is, roll you onto your side, all together... so we will be acting as a *splint* for you... OK? ...and I'm going to feel down your back. OK sir?

Beat

MAN

(*Indistinctly*) OK.

REG

It's very important you understand you don't make any movement yourself. If you've got any breaks you could damage your spinal cord. You - let *us* - move you. OK sir?

MAN

OK.

REG

OK team, get ready to log-roll...

(*Everyone places their hands at intervals along the man's body, the Reg holding the head.*)

On the count of three...

(*She raises her voice*) One. Two. *Three.*

(*Swiftly, the man is turned onto his side. The co-ordination of all the surgeons together, so they move as one, is impressive. Emily is watching, fascinated.*)

OK, how's that feeling, sir?

(*Beat*)

Now what I'm going to do, is feel down your back, and I want you to tell me if at any point I touch a tender point. OK?

(*Beat*)

All right, sir, here we go.

(*She starts to feel swiftly down his back, kneading gently with both hands.*)

Is that tender?

No?

And that?

And that?

That? (*The man winces and she immediately stops*)

Is that tender sir?

Beat

MAN

It's... no...

REG

It's not tender?

MAN

No.

REG

When I feel just there? (*She does so, delicately*) It's not tender?

MAN

(*Wincing*) No.

Beat

REG

(*Carefully*) If it's not tender... then why did you squeeze your eyes shut when I touched it?

MAN

Because... because of the sound it made.

Commotion outside. More doors banging. Another stretcher is brought in. It is a girl. One paramedic is wheeling, the other is performing chest compressions on the girl. Emily snaps to attention. As this scene unfolds, the surgeons continue examining their man, quietly.

PARAMEDIC

24-year-old girl, cardiac arrest, received fifteen minutes CPR in the ambulance...

(*Emily, Rebecca, the nurse and the anaesthetist are all readying themselves round the bed.*)

Been intubated... No past medical history.

EMILY

OK.

Activity on all sides. 20 seconds of CPR. They slide the girl off the ambulance trolley onto the A&E one. She is transferred from the ambulance 'life-pack' and connected onto the hospital's equipment: airbags/ventilator, defibrillator and drip. The 'dots' are ripped off her half-bare chest and replaced by the hospital stickies. The anaesthetist listens to the girl's chest. The nurse busies herself getting venous access. Emily is baring the girl's chest properly and doing the stickies.

EMILY

Can we check for an output... (*To the nurse*) Gel pads please.

Bilateral air entry?

ANAESTHETIST

Air entry but no respiratory effort, not a dicky bird.

EMILY

Somebody get her tympanic temperature (*the nurse busies herself with this, sticking a thermometer in the girl's ear*), somebody get venous access, a B.M. and gases please. I'll assess the rhythm. (*The nurse looks at the anaesthetist – both have their hands full*)

NURSE

'Somebody'?

Emily does not notice, she is looking at the screen to assess the rhythm of the heart.

ANAESTHETIST

(*To Rebecca, taking charge*) *You* do venous access, bloods and gases. (*Rebecca starts to take another sample of blood*)

EMILY

She's in V.F. So somebody get me the defibs please.

ANAESTHETIST

(*Craning to have a look*) No wait, that's asystole.

EMILY

It can't be asystole, it isn't totally flat.

ANAESTHETIST

That's just interference. No rhythm. She's flat as a pancake, take it from me.

EMILY

But if there's any doubt we should shock.

PARAMEDIC

(*A note of apology in his voice*) She's been flat for a while.

Small beat.

EMILY

Fine, let's not waste any more time. 1 milligram adrenalin please... 3 milligrams atropine... and somebody check for an /output.

ANAESTHETIST

(*Sharply*) /Don't say, '*somebody*'. It helps if you give the job to someone. Like her. (*He indicates Rebecca*)

EMILY

(*Taking this in*) Fine, you do pulse, *I'll* do adrenalin. (*She struggles to open the drugs while Rebecca obediently checks for a pulse*)

REBECCA

I don't think I can feel a pulse, do you want to check it?

EMILY

Fucking... *thing*. OK. You get on with these (*she hands Rebecca the un-opened needle pack*) I'm going to start three minutes chest compressions.

She starts to administer chest compressions.

Meanwhile, the surgeons are still examining their man.

REG

(*Raising her voice for the benefit of the team*)... So, no obvious signs of bleeding but we're dealing with bilateral calcanial fractures and a tibial fracture... OK team, getting ready to log roll again... on three...

One. Two. *Three.*

(*The man is turned again.*)

... James take a look at the back of his eyes...

(*James does so.*)

Mark, you're doing lines, please...

(*Mark busies himself setting up the 'lines' or drips for the man.*)

And let's have some x-rays.

The surgeons continue their survey of the man, quietly, as the x-ray machine is slowly wheeled over.

Emily has just reached the end of her cycle of CPR.

EMILY

Stop. Rhythm check –

ANAESTHETIST

Asystole.

EMILY

Are you *sure* that's asystole?

ANAESTHETIST

Yes, I'm sure! Her heart has stopped. Look at her. She's blue.

EMILY

Have you checked the leads? Have we turned up the gain?

ANAETHETIST

The gain is fine.

EMILY

Have we got a pulse?

ANAESTHETIST

(*Under his breath*) She's dead, for Christ's sake.

The nurse feels.

NURSE

No. –

EMILY

Tympanic temperature?

NURSE

34 degrees C tympanic.

EMILY

OK, can we get a bag of warmed Hartmann's.

NURSE

It'll take me a couple of minutes.

ANAESTHETIST

Worth it?

EMILY

Yes. We can try and warm her up.

(*The anaesthetist looks sceptical, but says nothing. The nurse goes. To Rebecca, who has just returned*) What's the gas?

REBECCA

She's acidotic. Ph 6.9.

EMILY

OK – bicarb please. Four H's, four T's – have we checked all reversible causes?

ANAESTHETIST

Yes.

EMILY

Anything else? Any traces of any drugs? Trackmarks? Heroin?

REBECCA

No. But let's give her the narcam, can't make her worse.

EMILY

Another milligram adrenalin, and 400 mikes of narcam.

REBECCA

What do you want first? Cos there's no... fucking bicarb here.

Emily opens a box in the drugs shelf of the arrest trolley. She does not find what she needs.

EMILY

Fuck's *sake*. OK, forget the bicarb, give her narcam and adrenalin.

3 minutes CPR. (*She starts chest compressions*)

The X-Ray machine is in place over the surgeons.

REG

Chest, lateral c-spine and pelvis.

(*The team take a token step away from the machine as the radiographer prepares to take the X-rays.*)

Are we ready.

RADIOGRAPHER

Ready.

(*The three x-rays are taken.*)

One.

Two.

Three. Now we'll have a clearer picture of what we've got inside.

And the team move in as one around the man again.

Emily's team has been joined by the nurse, and the Hartmanns has been hooked up to the girl's arm.

EMILY

(*Exhausted, she has just finished the last cycle of CPR*) Pulse check?

REBECCA

None.

EMILY

Rhythm check –

(*Unwillingly*) Asystole.

OK, I think we should try and shock her out of this now.

ANAESTHETIST

You're not going to shock her out of it, she's asystolic. It's not a shockable rhythm.

EMILY

What have we got to lose by shocking her?

ANAESTHETIST

It's not what the ALS guidelines say. I think we should go down the Asystole pathway.

EMILY

Which is what? We've tried everything else, we've got to do what we can to revert her out of it.

ANAESTHETIST

We're not going to get her 'out of it'. She's dead.

EMILY

(*Gives him a hard look, lifts the defibrillator paddles ready*) Everybody clear? Preparing to shock at 200.

ANAESTHETIST

Wrong paddles.

Emily wordlessly changes the paddles.

EMILY

Oxygen away, clear at the head, clear at the feet, clear at the sides, I'm clear, shocking at 200, go.

She shocks the girl. In a frozen moment 'out of time' she is not looking at the girl but up at the corner of the ceiling.

REBECCA

(*Baffled*) What?

EMILY

...

(*She collects herself, with difficulty*)

Pulse?

REBECCA

No pulse.

EMILY

What about the interference?

REBECCA

(*Looking at the monitor*) Totally flat. It's gone. Asystole.

Beat

EMILY

OK. So here we go. 3 minutes CPR. Rebecca, –

ANAESTHETIST

(*Turns to Emily*) I think we should stop.

EMILY

Stop?

ANAESTHETIST

The girl is dead. She was dead when she came in.

You've done everything you can.

EMILY

She's 24.

ANAESTHETIST

I know she's 24. I also know, she's dead.

EMILY

There was something there.

ANAESTHETIST

There was nothing there. It was interference.

(*To the others.*)

Any objections to stopping?

... OK, thank you everybody. Thank you. Thank you.

The team start to disperse. Emily speaks directly to the anaesthetist.

EMILY

I was meant to be leading that arrest. It's up to me to say when it's over.

ANAESTHETIST

You checked and treated all the reversible causes. There was nothing else we could do. You have to know when to say, enough.

(*Emily is silent.*)

We weren't going to get her back.

He carries on thanking, releasing everyone. As Emily's team breaks up and disperses around her, she takes a few steps towards the surgical team, watching their ballet, as they work as one, now moving their man once more onto a different bed to take him to theatre.

SURGICAL REG

... Everybody ready. All together now, team. One. Two. Three... That's it...

Emily's team have nearly all gone. She carries on watching.

SURGICAL REG

Great... all together now...

And the man is taken out of resuss, the surgeons moving as one. Then, they are gone. Emily sinks down onto a small wheeled chair.

Vashti has come in – to read a folder, in private. She does not register Emily slumped in the chair. A moment later, John comes in.

JOHN

Hi. Sorry, have I missed it?

(*Emily looks at him.*)

We had an arrest in CCU.

EMILY

Where were you when we needed you?

JOHN

What?

EMILY

I was leading that arrest. Where were you when I needed you?

JOHN

I told you, we had an arrest in CCU. I got here as soon as I could.

EMILY

Yeah, some 90-year-old, right? Well it wasn't a piece of 90-year old crud we got, you know, it was a 24-year-old girl.

Beat. Vashti is discreetly eavesdropping on their conversation.

JOHN

I didn't know she was 24. They said –

EMILY

I bet you fucking walked here, didn't you?

JOHN

What difference would it have made if I'd run?

EMILY

The anaesthetist decided to call it off. He wouldn't listen to me. You could have stopped him.

JOHN

What rhythm did she come in with?

EMILY

Asystole.

JOHN

Then the anaesthetist was right. She was dead on arrival.

EMILY

We had to do an arrest with one nurse, an anaesthetist, a house-officer, and half the drugs missing off the trolley. We weren't exactly giving her the benefit of the doubt, were we?

(*Beat*)

That is not an arrest team. And I shouldn't have been leading it. She didn't stand a chance.

(*She looks at John. He is expressionless.*)

What is wrong with you? You're the one who's fucking dead, you know that?

I was looking down at her and her face was this grey colour and all I could think was, that's me. She was my age.

Can you hear what I'm saying?

JOHN

Yes. I can hear what you're saying.

He turns on his heel and goes.

Vashti comes up to Emily

VASHTI

Try not to care so much. Not to care about the doctors, not to care about the patients.

Vashti goes.

Suddenly, the old lady, Gillian, is there, standing in her nightie. Throughout this next exchange she is extremely matter-of-fact, dispassionate.

GILLIAN

I thought you'd forgotten about me.

EMILY

(*Dully, automatically – she is miles away*) No, not forgotten about you.

(*Beat. She rouses herself.*)

Shouldn't you be in bed? What ward –

When did you get your speech back?

GILLIAN

Yesterday.

Beat

EMILY

Who's... who've we got looking after you now?

GILLIAN

I don't know.

EMILY

(*Going towards her, then stopping*) What ward have you come from?

Beat

GILLIAN

I don't want to be put in a box.

Beat

EMILY

I'm sure there won't be any need for that.

GILLIAN

You won't let them put me in a box.

EMILY

No.

GILLIAN

Who are all the people? (*She gestures round vaguely*) This room is *full* of people.

It is deserted.

EMILY

(*Puts a hand on her*) You should be in bed.

GILLIAN

They're all here. (*Looking directly at Emily*) They come and sit on my bed.

(*Confidentially*) I need to get back. He can't look after himself.

A nurse comes up.

NURSE

Come on darling, this isn't where we usually have our cocktail parties. You've had us all looking for you.

(*To Emily. In an undertone*) She's a bit confused.

GILLIAN

(*To Emily*) Don't forget about me.

EMILY

Of course not.

GILLIAN

I won't forget about you.

You've got a heavy gold chain around your neck.

(*Emily takes a step away from her, puts her hand up to her neck. There is only her stethoscope.*)

It doesn't suit you.

You've got cobwebs on your face.

It doesn't suit you.

NURSE

(*Gently but firmly leading her away*) Come on now, my love.

GILLIAN

(*Reassuringly*) I won't forget about you.

The nurse leads her away.

THE CONSULTANTS' OFFICE

Vashti sits, slumped, in a chair. Brian comes in.

BRIAN

I want to apologise, Vashti.

(*He doesn't register her state of mind. As he speaks she shows no reaction.*)

In your interview tomorrow they're going to bring up your conduct with the junior members of your team and ask you to justify it. Mark put in a bullying form against you, a month ago. I'm sorry. You should have complained to the consultants when you wanted. You would have got your story in first. Your instincts were right.

(*Beat*)

I gave you the wrong advice.

(*Beat*)

Vashti, your chances are still good because academically you're far and away the strongest candidate, I've had a look at the list. Play it right, it's yours. It's all in the playing.

(*Beat*)

All they want is –

VASHTI

A team player.

Beat.

BRIAN

Yes.

Finally Vashti speaks, flatly.

VASHTI

I'm interested in this 'team' business. What does it mean?

BRIAN

Being able to work together.

...Sharing responsibility...

...Getting on with people.

Beat.

VASHTI

Mark can't.

BRIAN

If Mark doesn't sort himself out then he'll damage his prospects too.

He'll screw things up for himself very nicely, don't you worry. He's not happy, poor sod. Half his problems stem from the fact that he didn't go to public school.

VASHTI

Yes.

(*Slowly*) You know, I think I'm a bit like Mark.

Thanks, Brian. For telling me.

BRIAN

That's OK.

(*He is disconcerted by her passivity.*)

Are you all right?

VASHTI

Who's going to be there in my interview?

BRIAN

The usual, plus a representative surgeon from a different specialty.

You know, for the sake of keeping it –

VASHTI

(*Interrupting*) Who's the representative surgeon.

BRIAN

Mr Milward.

(*Beat*)

Has something happened?

Beat

VASHTI

The funny thing is, Brian...

I *am* a team player. I wish I wasn't. Because if any one of my team fucks up, that's *my* fuck up. That's why I wouldn't let Mark finish stitching up after me that day. Because his crap scar belonged to me as well.

(*Beat*)

And right now, my aunt's lying in a bed, peritonitic, on Cowley ward, because not only Milward made a fuck up, but his whole team.

BRIAN

Your aunt?

VASHTI

Milward rogered her bile duct when he took her gall bladder out and nobody noticed that she was getting worse and worse, instead of better and better. I found out last night.

(*Beat*)

And then I found out that there was fuck all in the notes.

And then Mr Milward didn't answer any of my calls.

No one here *does* work together. They're all out hunting, for themselves.

BRIAN

... Don't let this affect your interview.

VASHTI

I won't let it affect my interview. But Mr Milward might.

(*Beat*)

I'm not going to hang about anymore. I'm going to go over his head. I'm going to get her transferred. I'm going to ring up my old consultant at Tommie's and get her transferred to a surgeon who knows what he's doing.

BRIAN

You can't.

VASHTI

I can. I just have to pick up the phone. It's not yet 5 o'clock. Prof'll still be there.

BRIAN

Vashti, this is suicide.

VASHTI

I read, in the BMJ, when we settle a score, the same neurones in our brain experience activity as the ones stimulated by eating something sugary. In other words, revenge *is* sweet.

BRIAN

You're losing your objectivity.

VASHTI

I think I lost it a long time ago.

What is it about this place that makes you into the opposite of what you are? Pretend you're a man if you're a woman, pretend you're English if you're Indian, I mean listen, listen to the voice I've invented for myself. It's like something out of *Jennings*. 'Jolly bad show!' I'm like Prof Bhatacharia, a poncy Indian man in a pin-striped suit with a watch on a chain who shuns everything Indian.

This place has hurt one of my family and I can't take it.

BRIAN

If you go over Milward's head and take your aunt out of this hospital then you can kiss that job goodbye.

VASHTI

If I don't, she'll die in that bed by the window. Because if you're a *real* team player in this place, you never take any responsibility for anything. You're part of a team so you're safe.

There are animals who are happy in this place, and animals who aren't.

I'm kissing goodbye to the job. I should have done it a long time ago.

She starts to dial in a phone.

EMILY'S ROOM

James sits on her bed, drinking a can of beer. Morning light streams through the window. He is watching daytime television – 'Doctors'. Emily comes in.

EMILY

What are you doing?

JAMES

What does it look like I'm doing? I'm having a beer and watching daytime television. 'Doctors,' to be precise.

EMILY

Why?

JAMES

Because I've just finished a night shift.

EMILY

So have I. Am I cracking open beers and watching shite?

(*Beat, filled with the dialogue from 'Doctors'.*)

I can't bear this.

(*She turns it off.*)

We didn't get her back.

JAMES

Who?

EMILY

A 24-year-old cardiac arrest.

JAMES

You win some, you lose some.

Emily sits, slowly.

EMILY

When we were trying to resuscitate her I looked up and I saw her. Up in the corner of the room. Just before she completely flat-lined. The anaethetist said there was no rhythm, that it was just interference.

Beat

JAMES

You're tired and freaked out.

Beat

EMILY

All through the rest of the night shift my shoulders were stiff and aching. I couldn't think why and then I realised. It was the CPR that I'd given that girl. I felt... dirty. She'd got into me. That dead girl.

(*Pause*)

...I thought I could do this job. I can't.

JAMES

You did your best.

He puts an arm around her. She detaches herself from him. She is crying properly, for the first time.

EMILY

No I didn't. I couldn't read the signs properly. I don't know why she died.

JAMES

We're not clairvoyant. The body's full of secrets. It doesn't always want to tell.

EMILY

Then it's your fault.

JAMES

No. Not always. We're just detectives, we look at the clues. Sometimes the arrows point in different directions.

EMILY

I felt that girl's rib break when I was giving her CPR.

JAMES

Things get mended, things get broken. It's like a car, you get in there and try to fix it.

EMILY

We were trying to bring a dead person back to life. And we couldn't.

She winces

JAMES

What's wrong?

EMILY

I don't know. A *pain.* In my back, in my chest. (*Her arms are wrapped around herself*)

JAMES

How long have you had it for?

EMILY

I don't know. I ache all over, all of the time, I feel dirty and sick all the time, I'm sick of the smell in this place, I hate breathing in the smell of shit on Care of the Elderly –

JAMES

So breathe through your mouth, that's what I do.

EMILY

Yeah, breathe through your mouth, wear gloves, stop listening when they're going on. Shut down, don't let them in.

JAMES

...Why have you got your arms like that?

EMILY

'To keep myself sterile.'

(*Beat*)

This place is making me sick. It stinks of death. It's making you sick too, James, you're drinking beer at nine in the morning.

JAMES

It isn't nine in the morning, as far as I'm concerned it's nine in the evening, I've just finished a hard day's work, I'm having a few beers, and I'm watching 'Doctors'. As my escape from reality.

EMILY

But it's not nine in the evening. You're upside down.

JAMES

I don't give a fuck. That's what I do when I finish a day's work. That's what *I* do. What, the girl went some place in the sky, that's in capital letters just slightly out of focus? This is *all bullshit.*

EMILY

Yeah. You've changed.

JAMES

...I can't believe you *actually* just said that.

EMILY

You go into this job because you care. To stay in it, you have to stop.

JAMES

And what does 'caring' mean, exactly? So someone dies and all you can think is that you're fucking hungry and when are you going to get the chance to eat that tuna baguette. So what? What we feel isn't some standardised A4 thing, Emily, it's torn up, bits, bobs, scraps, post-its. Whether you're a doctor or not. Don't go on about lacking the appropriate emotions because who has appropriate emotions anyway? If you think that makes us inhuman then you've got a fucking stupid idea of what being human is. And you haven't got the monopoly on it.

Pause

EMILY

Something's broken...like a tiny cog inside a clock that's jammed... and I can't mend it.

(*Pause*)

I slept with somebody else.

Beat

JAMES

Who?

EMILY

Mark.

JAMES

Why?

EMILY

Because he wanted to.

Beat

JAMES

...You fucking idiot.

EMILY

Because we're finished. It's a weird feeling, it's just outside the frame, but it's a massive fracture, bleeding internally.

JAMES

Why *him*?

EMILY

It's not about him. Nothing more is going to happen with him. It's because you stop caring out there and you stop caring in here, the traffic is two way, the one bleeds into the other.

JAMES

Please please please don't use that *fucking* word again!

EMILY

What word?

JAMES

Care! How do you know I don't care?

Beat

EMILY

It hurts. Here. (*Her chest*)

Beat

JAMES

So see a doctor.

He leaves.

THE WARD

Morning. Sunlight. Vashti stands irresolutely. Holding a purple form. It is obvious she has been crying. The middle-aged nurse, Olga, walks by, sees her.

OLGA

(*She double-takes*) ...Is everything all right?

VASHTI

It's nothing.

OLGA

Have you been...

Vashti blows her nose.

VASHTI

No... No. It's... my aunt. She's not very well.

OLGA

Your aunt? What's happened?

VASHTI

Nothing...

OLGA

Oh I am sorry, what...

VASHTI

(*Swallowing down tears*) No, no, it's fine. It's boring.

There's just some things I've got to do before I go.

OLGA

Go?

A beat while Vashti tries to regain composure.

VASHTI

It's a long story. I'm going on leave, and before I go, I've got to... finish everything off here... (*She gestures, off*)... I'd better get on with this. It's the last thing I've got to do.

OLGA

Oh. – The purple form. For Mr Mercer.

VASHTI

Yes. I'm waiting to go in...

Vashti takes a deep breath, unfolds the purple form.

OLGA

We're not going to see him on the telly again, are we?

VASHTI

No.

I've got to decide whether to tell him or not. That we've reached the end of the line.

I don't think he's going to want to know.

Pause

OLGA

So will you tell him?

Beat

VASHTI

Only if he wants to be told.

Beat. Olga is looking at Vashti closely.

OLGA

Do you want me to go in with you?

Beat.

VASHTI

Yes please.

CARDIOLOGY

Emily and John together. Emily is sitting, John is standing, with a stethoscope. He has a new dressing on his neck.

JOHN

...How would you describe it?

EMILY

A dullness...

(*He puts his stethoscope to Emily's chest.*)

What can you hear in there?

Pause.

JOHN

I can hear... lots of things...

I can hear your heart...

John removes the stethoscope from Emily's chest. Looks at her.

Stressed?

Beat.

EMILY

Is it my heart?

JOHN

I don't think it's your heart.

(*Pause*)

What you're feeling there is probably what we call, ghost pain, or phantom pain...

My guess is you've damaged some nerves in your neck, I don't know how... And these nerve endings supply other parts of your body, like here... (*Her chest*) or here for instance, your hand... (*Indicates her hand*) And they're telling you there's a pain there when there isn't.

EMILY

A false alarm.

JOHN

Kind of.

Beat.

EMILY

(*Indicating the dressing on his neck*) What's that?

JOHN

Oh... had to have a little procedure done. Just waiting for the all clear now.

EMILY

Nothing serious?

JOHN

No. Like you. Nothing serious.

He gently takes her hand in his.

JOHN

You can feel – when I do this? (*He runs a finger down the side of her hand*)

EMILY

...Yes.

JOHN

Any numbness – down these two fingers here?

Beat.

EMILY

No...

JOHN

But you're a nervous person...

EMILY

How do you know?

JOHN

(*Holds up her hand*) You bite your nails...

(*Pause. They look at each other.*)

You're feeling a pain... but it's just a ghost. It doesn't exist.

EMILY

But if I can feel it, it exists.

JOHN

So take something to stop feeling it. Tell your body a little white lie. That's what we're good at here.

(*Pause*)

You think you can't do the job. But we have to do the job.

I thought I couldn't do it. I thought I was dying.

EMILY

How do you feel now?

Beat.

JOHN

Alive.

THE WARD

Vashti and Olga are with Mr Mercer, who we now see lying in a bed. He is much more wasted than he was in Act One – very ill. Throughout this scene Vashti is different to how we have seen her before. Very warm; very kind.

VASHTI

Mr Mercer!

MR MERCER

Doctor!

VASHTI

How are you?

MR MERCER

All the better for seeing you...

VASHTI

Listen to him...

(*They laugh.*)

He's a terrible flirt!

Well, Mr Mercer, I just wanted to pop in on you, and... See how you were doing... I see we've still got you on the gentamicin...

MR MERCER

Yes...

VASHTI

Right... (*She looks at the chart at the end of his bed*) But he's off the clexane injections?

OLGA

Yes. Came off them a week ago.

VASHTI

(*Continuing to look at the chart*) Good. Good. That's... all as it should be.

MR MERCER

(*There is something urgent in his voice*) But... how am I doing?

VASHTI

Well –

MR MERCER

I mean, how am I doing *now*, doctor?

VASHTI

(*She takes his hand, squeezes it*) You're doing very well.

MR MERCER

But am I doing any better?

(*Beat*)

I need to know the truth.

I need you to be honest.

Beat. Vashti nods.

VASHTI

Mr Mercer...

We have no drug that can control your cancer now.

(*Beat*)

All we can do is keep your symptoms at bay.

(*Pause*)

So the question now is, Mr Mercer, what *you* want.

(*Beat*)

Because...what we want now is to make this as easy as we can for you.

(*Pause*)

Do you understand?

Beat.

MR MERCER

Am I dying?

VASHTI

...Yes.

MR MERCER

How long?

Beat.

VASHTI

I can't tell you that. I don't know.

All I would suggest... What I would suggest, is that, what we do now is... we just... leave you alone.

(*Pause*)

Leave you in peace.

(*Pause*)

No more drip.

No more antibiotics.

No more taking your pulse and temperature.

Because... I think we've reached the end of the road with all that.

I think we've finished with all that now.

(*Olga silently nods.*)

Do you agree?

(*A pause*)

And if your heart were to stop beating...

I don't think we should try and start it again.

If you'd like us to, we could try.

But I don't think we should.

Pause

MR MERCER

No.

Beat.

VASHTI

So we're agreed on that?

MR MERCER

Yes.

Beat.

VASHTI

And now the most important thing – for us – is that you're comfortable.

And we'll do everything we can to make that happen.

(*Pause. She squeezes his hand.*)

Mr Mercer.

(*Pause*)

We're all very proud of you.

And we'll all be here.

Geoffrey. You've done so well.

And that's me being completely honest with you.

(*Beat*)

I'll be in again soon.

She is about to leave but he stops her.

MR MERCER

Thank you doctor.

Beat.

VASHTI

That's a pleasure.

MR MERCER

No, thank you.

VASHTI

That's a pleasure.

That's what we're here for.

She goes. Olga follows her out of the room and immediately, outside the room, Vashti crumples into tears. Olga puts a hand on her shoulder.

VASHTI

I had to tell him. I had to tell him.

And around her, the sounds of the hospital engulf us, as once more, we see the doctors, but not the patients they are referring to:

REBECCA

(*To no one in particular*) I've got a lady, 65, no known cardiac history, presenting complaint chest pains, can I refer her to one of the medics please?

BRIAN

(*Urgently, pushing his head round a door*) /OK, she's arrested, can we put out a crash call please?

The assorted alarms of the crash call sound out. The same flurry of activity.

LAKSHMI

(*Her voice amplified over a tannoy*) Can we have an SHO in resuss now, /please?

A bed is wheeled through the doors, people around it so we cannot see who is in it.

ANAESTHETIST

(*At the head of the bed, he is wearing surgical hat and scrubs*) / What's her history? Does anyone know what drugs she's on? We need to know who's leading this arrest!

REBECCA

(*Arriving at the bed*) *I'm* leading this arrest!

The defibrillator has arrived at the bedside.

ROSIE

There are too many people round this bed!

Everyone ignores her.

REBECCA

(*Holding pads aloft*) I'm clear, clear at the end, clear at the sides, everyone clear, oxygen away, shocking at 200, go!!

She plunges the pads down and shocks. There are so many people standing round the bed now we can't see what is happening.

Mark stands a little distance away, looks at the knot of activity.

MARK

I don't run to arrests anymore. I take my time.

He watches them.

REBECCA

Stop.

Rhythm check.

BRIAN

Asystole.

No pulse.

REBECCA

1 mg adrenalin. 3 mg atropine. Start chest compressions again / please –

Everyone perspiring, chest compressions taking place.

MARK

I mean it's not like you're going to save anyone's life, or anything, is it?

He watches them.

BRIAN

/We need more oxygen here –

LAKSHMI

I'll get it –

ANAESTHETIST

I don't think we're winning here –

MARK

Five minutes...and it's all over.

He watches them.

REBECCA

(*Suddenly stepping back*) OK, OK, OK, everybody.

(*Beat*)

Thank you.

I'm not certain this is in the best interests of the patient.

Any objections to calling this off?

(*Slowly, everyone straightens up from the bed. It is empty.*)

Does anyone object if we stop now?

(*Everyone murmurs assent. Rebecca turns to each person in turn.*)

Thank you. Thank you. Thank you. Thank you. Thank you.

Thank you, every body.

Thank you.

The empty bed is wheeled off. Left behind them on the empty stage, a solitary hospital porter, a metre-wide broom in front of him, pushes the pile of the debris from the failed cardiac arrest across the stage: bubble wrapping, tubes, plastic shrink-packaging.

Mark watches him go. Then turns and goes himself.

CURTAIN